PUERTO RICAN MUSIC FOLLOWING THE SPANISH AMERICAN WAR

1898: The Aftermath of the Spanish American War and Its Influence on the Musical Culture of Puerto Rico

Catherine Dower

D1600345

UNIVERSITY
PRESS OF
AMERICA

LANHAM • NEW YORK • LONDON

Copyright © 1983 by

University Press of America,™ Inc.

4720 Boston Way
Lanham, MD 20706

3 Henrietta Street
London WC2E 8LU England

Library of Congress Cataloging in Publication Data

Dower, Catherine, 1924–
    Puerto Rican music following the Spanish American
War.

    Bibliography: p.
    Includes index.
    1. Music – Puerto Rico – 20th century – History and
criticism. I. Title.
ML207.P8D7   1983   781.77295   83–10290
ISBN 0–8191–3333–7
ISBN 0–8191–3334–5 (pbk.)

PREFACE

In 1973 while searching choir lofts in San Juan, Puerto Rico for evidence of music from earlier centuries, I found instead music from the first decade of the twentieth century. When I announced my discovery to Donald Thompson, Professor of Music of the University of Puerto Rico, he was elated with the prospect of music from the early 1900s but disbelieving that the music manuscripts dated from the period following the Spanish American War. He told me that composers were not active during this era because of the economic and cultural regression. Evidence proved otherwise.

The purpose of this book is to present a survey of the cultural activities that occurred in Puerto Rico following 1898--the American Occupation of the Island. To this end, the author has also included information related to the economic and cultural regression, an explanation of the American military "take over," and the appointment to Puerto Rico of the one United States appointed official who was well accepted by the Puerto Ricans. Musical activities included in the study are the Ateneo Puertorriqueño festivities, religious feast day observances, band concerts, public school programs, and the activities of well known Puerto Rican composers of that day.

During this era many opera companies visited Puerto Rico, and most of these performed in the Municipal Theatre in San Juan. These theatrical activities have been well described by Emilio J. Pasarell in Origines y Desarrollo de la Afición Teatral en Puerto Rico I (1951) and II (1967).

Only those church services with instrumental ensembles are noted because church services were so numerous, and it is my intention to show that the instrumental tradition was carried on in the churches at this time.

The author expresses her gratitude to Professor Donald Thompson for his assistance and to his wife, music librarian and Professor of Music of the University of Puerto Rico, Annie Thompson, for placing her most helpful bibliography at my disposal before publication; to Héctor Campos Parsi, former Music Director of the Instituto de Cultura

iii

Puertorriqueña, for his much valued direction and to the present Music Director, Vanessa Vassallo and the Executive Director, Dr. Leticia del Rosario, for permission to reprint photographs from the Institute of Puerto Rican Culture Photographic Department and music from the General Archives of Puerto Rico; to Ricardo Morla and his sister, Angelina Morlá, for allowing me to visit several times the private collection of their father's music; to Genoveva De Arteaga for lending materials to me and for the many interviews she gave me; to Professor José A. Balseiro for permission to use his father's picture and music, and to Vincent Shields for providing materials for me to use.

To the many librarians--without whose assistance my job would have been nearly impossible--at the University of Puerto Rico, Rio Piedras, the Ateneo Puertorriqueño, Archivo General de Puerto Rico, Carnegie Library in San Juan, the Library of Congress Newspaper and Periodical Room as well as the Main Reading Room and Music Division, the Lincoln Center Library for the Performing Arts, the National Archives, Amherst College Library, Smith College Library, especially Mrs. Mary Ankudovich, Music Librarian; Mrs. Pauline Collins, Latin American Acquisitions Librarian of the Univerity of Massachusetts, and the many librarians at Westfield State College, especially Mrs. Catherine Handy, Reference Librarian, Katherine Higgins, Cataloguer, and Mr. Kenneth Cotton, Head Librarian, and the Westfield State College Computer Center, especially Debbie Cushing for her special help with the Wang Word Processor, to Susan Burns, '84, and José Efrain Martínez, President of the Hispanic Institute, Inc. of Holyoke, I wish to give my heartiest appreciation.

I am especially indebted to my colleague Professor Martin Kaufman who carefully read the entire manuscript and made suggestions for revisions, and I give my utmost appreciation and thanks to my mother and brother, without whose assistance none of this would be possible.

                              Catherine A. Dower

Holyoke, Massachusetts
March 22, 1983

TABLE OF CONTENTS

vi

ILLUSTRATIONS

Page

CHAPTER I

THE NINETEENTH CENTURY MUSICAL TRADITION

In 1898, during the Spanish American War, American troops invaded Puerto Rico and raised the American flag. To many Puerto Ricans, it was apparent that the almost 400 years of cultural exchange with Spain had come to an end. According to some musicians and writers, the arrival of Americans signalled the beginning of a period of decline. The musical tradition which had been developing during the nineteenth century, it was argued, declined during the period following the War. In the leading historical study written during this era (1915), Fernando Callejo insisted that in the aftermath of the war came an economic depression which discouraged opera companies from coming to the island and which resulted in the stagnation of music during the period.[1] Later writers agreed with that assessment, always citing Callejo as evidence. In 1952, Carmen Gómez Tejera published an article which was written as a section of a high school textbook, and using Callejo as a source described a general decline in art and music during the era.[2] Another writer, María Luisa Muñoz, who was a leading music teacher of the island, declared that the cultural life in Puerto Rico, which had scarcely begun, would soon disappear.[3] Although her text has carried the Callejo text into the twentieth century additions and corrections up to 1915 were not made. Rather interestingly, each of these authors provided information on prominent musicians during the first decade of the twentieth century, but they overlooked the extensive musical activities of those years. Therefore, there has been a complete neglect of the activities of this period.

During the nineteenth century, Puerto Rican musical tradition had been developing, as the Spanish heritage was slowly assimilated into Afro-Caribbean folk music. With the arrival of well-known artists, military bands, and opera companies all trained in Europe, the cultural life of the island began to be transformed. When many of these musicians remained in Puerto Rico and established themselves as music teachers, they played a major role in the musical development of the region.

1

Each Spanish military company had a band, consisting of some very fine musicians. Battalions from Asturia, Iberia, Granada, and Madrid were stationed on the island, and their bands not only played at military and civic affairs but they also entertained the public with a series of concerts. Some of these musicians decided to remain in Puerto Rico when their units were ordered back to Spain, and they became leading music teachers of the period. The musical director of the Granada Regiment, José Álvarez, remained in Puerto Rico and became a teacher of some of the island's foremost nineteenth century musicians, including Felipe Gutiérrez y Espinosa. In addition, in 1840 one of the clarinetists in the Álvarez band, Juan Inés Ramos, himself became a teacher in Arecibo. Two of his sons, Adolfo Heraclio and Federico Ramos, became noted composers. Even in the previous century, an official band contributed to the musical culture of the island by playing at dances as well as before church groups. This was the fife and drum corps of the El Fijo Battalion, which was organized in 1765 by Field Marshall Alejandro O'Reilly when he was Governor.[4]

In addition to the military bands, a number of well-known foreign musicians and singers gave concerts in Puerto Rico during the nineteenth century, contributing to the island's cultural development. Two of the most notable artists with international reputations arrived together in 1857--Louis Moreau Gottschalk (1829-1869), virtuoso pianist from New Orleans, and Adelina Patti (1843-1919), a fourteen year old singer.[5] During each performance in Ponce, Patti sang arias from well-known operas, and Gottschalk played his own piano arrangements accompanied by prominent local musicians.[6] Gottschalk may have exerted an influence on the style of Puerto Rican music and two of his compositions written at that time, Souvenir de Puerto Rico (Marche des Gibaros) and Danza, both echoed Puerto Rican folk-lore characteristics.

There was also a noticeable influence by Italian opera of the Romantic Era. In May of 1835, an Italian Philharmonic Company presented the first opera ever staged in Puerto Rico, a performance of Rossini's Barber of Seville.[7] In 1842 another Italian opera company arrived after a visit to Cuba. Under the direction of Stéfano Busatti, it presented a series of operas by Bellini, Donizetti, and Rossini.[8] Busatti perhaps fell in love with the climate and beauty of the Caribbean and decided to remain on the island as a music teacher. In 1848, he organized an opera troupe with the cooperation of the well-known Catalonian musician, Félix Astol Artes (1811-1901), who himself had emigrated to San Germán in that year also by way of Cuba.[9] This gave Puerto Rican musicians their first opportunity to perform in an opera. In 1877, the Petrillo Opera Company from Italy came to San Juan and performed La Traviata under the direction of Rosario Aruti, who also remained on the island and became a music teacher.[10]

According to the Boletín Mercantil de Puerto Rico, a number of other teachers came to the island. In 1839, Marcellino Castillo announced that he had twenty years' of experience and that he wanted to continue teaching music theory.[11] The same year, José Bermejo, a piano teacher, opened an academy of solfeo-canto-piano.[12] Two years later, José Cabrizas, another recent arrival advertised that he wanted to purchase a piano of good quality and that soon he would be teaching on the island.[13] Later that year Professor Carlos Gola announced that he was looking for a studio and that he was planning to import music and sell it at a small profit.[14] The following year, a ballet teacher arrived.[15]

With the arrival of opera companies, well-known foreign musicians and teachers contributed a unique classical component to the Puerto Rican culture. As early as 1832, a Philharmonic Society was in existence, continuing for a few years, disbanding, and then being revived in 1845.[16] A municipal theatre opened in that same year, with a concert by the English tenor, William Pearman.[17] In 1856, the Philharmonic Society of Puerto Rico awarded a prize to Felipe Gutiérrez y Espinosa (1825-1899), for the first opera composition by a Puerto Rican composer. The opera in three acts, Guarionex, was based on a libretto, La Palma del Cacique (Madrid, 1852) by Alejandro Tapia, about a Hispaniola leader who fought against Christopher Columbus.[18] The music consisted of a combination of arias and choruses, much like the Italian oratorios of the same period.

Gutiérrez was one of several outstanding Puerto Rican musicians of the nineteenth century, all of whom died before or at the onset of the "critical years" following the Spanish American War. His Father, Julián, had been a musician with the Granada Regiment which came to the island in 1815. With Sandalio Callejo (1833-1883), a distinguished professor of music, Felipe Gutiérrez formed a musical society intended to raise the cultural level and to gain recognition for the art of music. On January 26, 1871, Gutiérrez requested that the governor-general establish an Academy of Music. When the request was granted, he asked the governor to subsidize a building and to pay for supplies, declaring that the academy already had 360 students and that some local groups were in need of adequate facilities for performances.[19]

Gutiérrez was primarily a composer of sacred music; in 1858 he became Maestro de Capilla of the Cathedral of San Juan, a position he held for some forty years. He had a great knowledge of Gregorian Chant and incorporated it into his music, utilizing the plainsong themes in his religious works. He was a prolific, spontaneous composer whose works were influenced by the works of Italian composers. He was severely criticized for composing sentimental music that was distracting to the congregation. He then made a drastic change, and began to write in an instrumental style. This transformation has been described as a fatal mistake, as the melodic form was sacrificed.[20] This had been his greatest asset, but he completely reversed his style, writing music that was more symphonic than religious. Indeed, the Gloria and Credo of his last masses were almost sonatas for orchestra with vocal accompaniment. In addition, his orchestra usually included two trumpets, two clarinets, and a bombardino, and it lacked violas, oboes, and bassoons. It had a proportion of six wind instruments to five stringed instruments, and the result was an unbalanced sound—overpowered by the stronger wind instruments. Although he was advised to substitute an oboe for the second clarinet, a bassoon for the bombardino, and violin and viola for the two trumpets, Gutiérrez was implacable. His later work had become extremely bold, and he lost favor with the people as well as with the head of the cathedral, all of whom wanted softer, more "religious" music than he was providing. In 1898, his position was terminated and he was retired on a small pension. He died the following year; his inglorious ending of a great career made him a forgotten figure. Indeed, his death date has been consistently recorded as 1900, instead of the correct date: November 27, 1899.[21]

Another musician who exerted an influence on the island's musical culture was Adolfo Heraclio Ramos y Buensont (1837-1891). He was a brilliant pianist-composer who had been favorably compared to Franz Liszt. Born in Arecibo, he studied under the direction of his father, Juan Inés Ramos, a member of the band of the regiment of Granada, and a German teacher whose name was Alfred Mello, with whom he studied composition and piano. Ramos had exceptionally large hands, permitting a span of an eleventh on the keyboard. He preferred brilliant music, difficult passages, and he specialized in the execution of variations and fantasies. Although he produced only a few published works, they have been compared with those of Gottschalk. In the first Feria Exposition held in Puerto Rico (1854), Ramos received a silver medal for his work, Fantasía con Variaciones Sobre la Polka de Jenny Lind. In 1860's Exposition, he received a gold medal for his piano composition, Variaciones Sobre el Carnaval de Venecia. In 1865 he received a prize for his Fantasía Sobre Motivos del Himno Inglés, God Save the King. He was a musician of international fame, having participated in the Saint Cecilia contest in Rome, where he won a gold medal and diploma of honor for his piano fantasy, El Ave en el Desierto, and honorable mention for his Didactic Studies for octaves. He also won gold medals and diplomas of honor in his native country, and although he held a prominent place among the musicians of his day, he died poor and almost unknown to the general public.[22]

The first Puerto Rican composer to cultivate the pianistic danza as salón music was Manuel Gregorio Tavárez (1843-1883). He began his musical studies with José Cabrizas, a Catalonian musician who had settled in San Juan; he also studied organ with Domingo Delgado, organist at the Cathedral. His talent was recognized, and in 1857 he received a scholarship to study at the Paris Conservatoire. In 1858 he studied harmony and composition with Professor Daniel Auber, Director of the Conservatoire, and piano with Eugène D'Albert and Alphonse Laurent. Unfortunately, he lost the use of his left arm becoming partially paralyzed and was forced to terminate his studies and return to Puerto Rico. He settled in Ponce, which had become the musical center of the island, and he dedicated his life to teaching. Tavárez was an extraordinary teacher who was able to bring out the best in his

students, and who was able to develop all their
skills. He was able to overcome his physical
problems, but it was reported that only the more
advanced pupils seemed to profit from his teaching;
others were unable to overlook the paralysis in his
arm.

Tavárez composed a collection of danzas, a
musical form which was thought to have been the
successor of the Spanish contradanza and Cuban
habanera brought to Puerto Rico by General Aristegui
in 1844. The danza is a couples' dance suitable for
small social gatherings. The works of Tavárez were
instrumental in establishing the danza as an
instrumental form in Puerto Rico. His favorite
composer was Chopin, whose works were known to have
had a great influence on his development. In fact,
Chopin's Ballade in G Minor served as a model for
Tavárez, who was also influenced by Gottschalk.
Tavárez's march for the piano, ¡Redención! is modeled
after a work which Gottschalk dedicated to the
Emperor of Brazil.[23] Tavárez's La Marcha Triunfal
Redención won first prize, a gold medal, at the
Feria Exposition of 1882.[24] In 1881, it was
published in Spain by Andrés Vidal Roger, and several
copies are preserved in the Archivo General de Puerto
Rico.[25] When he died, the townspeople of Ponce
covered their balconies with shrouds and abstained
from playing the piano. The day of mourning was
evidence of their deep love for their native son. It
was reported that only one of his pupils, Francisco
(Paco) Cortés, then a child, dared play the piano as
the funeral procession passed the Ponce Casino. He
played Tavárez's patriotic march ¡Redención! Although
he was dead, Tavárez's influence remained--many of
his students became outstanding musicians with an
important impact on the future development of music
in Puerto Rico. Among these were Juan Morel Campos,
Francisco Cortés, and Gonzalo Núñez.

Juan Morel Campos (1857-1896) was recognized as
Tavárez's protégé. Campos was influenced by the music
of the Italian artists who performed in Puerto Rico,
as well as by his master and teacher. Although best
known for his danzas, he also wrote about 60 pieces
of church music, including masses, litanies, salves,
choruses, and prayers; he also composed zarzuelas
(Spanish type operas with dialogue). Morel Campos
first studied solfeggio and violin with Antonio
Egipciaco, and then worked with Tavárez, who

6

introduced him to composition and to the study of harmony. His knowledge of instrumentation came from his experience in the band of the Batallón de Cazadores de Madrid; he was soloist on the bombardino. Morel Campos contributed to the music of the region, although his first danzas were not richly harmonic, nor did they have embellishments. His later music immortalized him, as he immortalized the danza: he composed over 280 danzas! He continued the danza tradition, enriching the form with harmonic combinations, new rhythms, and composing danzas for orchestra. His Sinfonía La Lira won a gold medal at the 1882 Ponce Feria Exposition. Later he was awarded a diploma of honor for his march, Juegos florales, which triumphed at the Casino of Mayagüez (1895).[26] At the Ateneo Puertorriqueño contest of 1893, he won a prize of 100 pesos for his orchestral symphony, Puerto Rico Sinfonía a gran orquesta, con reminiscensias de aires populares Puertorriqueños.[27]

He was an exceptionally talented instrumentalist, proficient on the flute, contra bass, and bombardino. He also improvised on the organ, but was more proficient on the piano. He organized an orchestra in Ponce and was known as one of the country's finest directors of bands and orchestras. He even directed a zarzuela company that toured South America and he organized and directed the Banda de Bomberos (Firemen) of Ponce. On April 26, 1896, Morel Campos was conducting the theatre orchestra at La Perla in Ponce, while the zarzuela company of Lloret and Pastor were preparing to present El reloj de Lucerna. Tragically, after the overture, Morel Campos suffered a heart attack and collapsed at the podium. Because his life was so short, he left few successors. His music is still widely performed, however, and remains a favorite on Latin American concert programs.[28]

NOTES

1. Fernando Callejo Ferrer. *Música y Músicos Portorriqueños.* San Juan: Tip. Cantero Fernández & Co., 1915; reprinted as *Música y Músicos Puertorriqueños.* Amaury Veray, ed. San Juan: Editorial Coquí, 1971, pp. 67-70 of Chapter IV, "1898-1014." Any pages referred to in the notes of this study relate to the 1971 edition.

2. Carmen Gómez Tejera in "Arte Puertorriqueño,"*Programma de Español,* II. Hato Rey, P.R.: Editorial del Departamento de Instrucción Pública, 1952, p. 99.

3. María Luisa Muñoz. *La música en Puerto Rico: Panorama histórico-cultural.* Sharon, Conn.: Troutman Press, 1966, p. 136. Similar statements may also be found by Fernando Caso, in *Héctor Campos Parsi in the History of Twentieth Century Music of Puerto Rico.* Bloomington, Indiana: Indiana University Master of Music thesis, 1972, pp. 3-4.

4. Robert M. Fitzmaurice. *Music Education in Puerto Rico: A Historical Survey with Guidelines for an Exemplary Curriculum.* Tallahasse, Florida: Florida State University Ph.D. dissertation, 1970, p. 48. Muñoz, p. 10, gives the names as Domingo O'Reilly and the date as 1756. She appears to have taken her information from Callejo, p. 39. Until 1974, the San Juan Cathedral choir loft possessed a termite eaten 1790 Register of the El Fijo Batallón, *Libro de las parridas de confirmaciones terrecientes a los tres Batallón del Regimento Fijo de Puerto Rico.* It was the oldest dated book in the choir loft and was the only book remaining after the church music was supposedly transferred to the Archives of the Archbishop in 1975. The music has now seemingly disappeared (1976). A memorial article on El Fijo Batallón appeared in *Boletín Mercantil de Puerto Rico* [from now on to be abbreviated as *BM*] LXI/92 (April 19, 1899), 1.

5. Emilio J. Pasarell. "El centenario de los conciertos de Adelina Patti y Louis Moreau Gottschalk en Puerto Rico," *Revista del Instituto de Cultura Puertorriqueña,* II/2 (January/March, 1959), 52-55. Also see the same author's *Origenes y desarrollo de la afición teatral en Puerto Rico,* I. Río Piedras: Editorial Universitaria [Universidad de Puerto Rico] 1951, pp. 140-148.

6. *Ibid.*, p. 145. Among musicians who assisted them were Carlos Allard, brother of Delfín Allard, director of the Paris Conservatoire and Gregorio Ledesma, Ponce pianist.

7. La Gaceta del Gobierno de Puerto Rico, IV/61 (May 21, 1835), 244.

8. BM, XL/58 (May 18, 1842), 319-320.

9. La Gaceta del Gobierno de Puerto Rico, XVII/74 (June 20, 1848), 4. Later he composed La Borinqueña, which has been the national hymn of Puerto Rico since July 25, 1952.

10. Pasarell. Orígenes y desarrollo . . . . I, pp. 152-3.

11. BM, No. 24, p. 192.

12. Ibid., No. 32, p. 256. He advertised in three subsequent issues, June 26, No. 33, p. 264; June 27, No. 34, p. 272; and June 29, No. 35, p. 288, and apparently met his quota.

13. Ibid., No. 205, p. 103. His advertisements appeared only once, on February 7, 1841, p. 111.

14. Ibid., No. 245, p. 423.

15. Ibid., No. 11, p. 88. He advertised only once more, on February 9, 1842, p. 95.

16. "El Origen del Teatro Tapia," Angela Luisa, Revista gráfica de Puerto Rico, V/51 (July, 1971), 58.

17. Ibid.

18. See Robert M. Stevenson. A Guide to Caribbean Music History. Lima, Peru: Ediciones "CVLTVRA," 1975, pp. 11f and 12c.

19. Callejo, p. 54. Callejo cites the Archivo Municipal de San Juan (1871-77) Legado 57—Expediente No. 33. Also see Centenario de la Fundación del Ateneo Puertorriqueño 1876-1976. San Juan: Ateneo Puertorriqueño, 1976, n.p. in which he is mentioned as the founder of the Ateneo.

20. Compositores Puertorriqueños. San Juan: Archivo General de Puerto Rico, Unpublished booklet, p. 5.

21. According to Puerto Rico: Estado Libre Asociado de Puerto Rico, Departamento de Salud: Acta de Defunción, No. 413 (November 28, 1899), information kindly sent to me by Gustavo Batista. Also see announcement of the corrected date in El Mundo, LVI/84 (May 11, 1975), 4-5, and the death notice in El País, V/280 (November 29, 1899), 2. He left over 300 works many of which are preserved in the Archivo General de Puerto Rico. Thirty manuscripts are owned by Gustavo Batista, mandolinist, of San Juan.

22. Católogo de obras musicals (1953). Archivo General de Puerto Rico Reference Room, No. 1465. His works are in the Music Section, Nos. 1463-1474.

23. Grande Fantasie triomphale sur l'hymn national bresilien, Op. 69 (1869).

24. According to José Ramón Abad. Puerto Rico en la feria exposición de Ponce en 1882. San Juan: Editorial Coquí, 1967, p. 87.

25. The Archivo General de Puerto Rico possesses many of his works. Nos.1737-1902, including songs, waltzes, and danzas.

26. Callejo, pp. 128-130, notes that for the same work he was awarded (posthumously) a bronze medal and diploma at the Buffalo Exposition in 1901. Juegos florales had been submitted as representative of Puerto Rican music and received honorable mention at Buffalo according to The San Juan News, VI/238 (October 12, 1901), 7.

27. Ateneo Puertorriqueño. San Juan: Talleres Gráficos Interamericanos, Inc., 1966, n.p.

28. His manuscripts are preserved in the Archivo General de Puerto Rico in the Colecciones Amaury Veray, Antonio Otero, Ernesto Ramos-Antonini, Graham, José Hernández Bosch, Monserrate Deliz, as well as in the Ponce Museum. The Ponce works are catalogued at the Archivo General Reference Room. His danzas have been published by the Instituto de Cultura Puertorriqueña: Album de danzas de Juan Morel Campos. 5 vols., San Juan, 1957, and are recorded by Jesús María Sanromá. San Juan: Instituto de Cultura Puertorriqueña, Nos. I CP-AD.

CHAPTER II

THE ECONOMIC AND CULTURAL REGRESSION

The four composers--Felipe Gutiérrez, Adolfo Heraclio Ramos, Manuel Gregorio Tavárez, and Juan Morel Campos--were active late in the nineteenth century and all died before 1900. Their departure from the scene certainly contributed to the description of the early twentieth century as a period of cultural regression in Puerto Rico. Furthermore, other musicians who could have carried on the tradition had already left the island for various reasons. Among them were Gonzalo Núñez, Antonio Paoli, and Francisco P. Cortés.

Gonzalo Núñez (ca. 1850-1915), who was born in Bayamón, first studied under José Cabrizas, a leading Catalonian musician. Then after working with Tavárez and Morel Campos. he attended the Paris Conservatoire where he studied with Georges Mathias and Félix LeCouppey. In 1873, he won first prize in piano at the Conservatoire.[1] When he left Paris, in 1875, he settled in New York instead of Puerto Rico. He became a piano teacher, but he also demonstrated his ability on concert tour. When he appeared in Steinway Hall in New York, the music critic of <u>The New York Times</u> wrote:

> "Equally brilliant, tasteful and . . . . thoughtful playing has not been listened to in a long while . . . . In . . . all these places he supplied evidence of considerable feeling and a thorough mastery of technique . . . . It will be pleasant and edifying to hear Señor Núñez again, and if renders what we may call sentimental music as skillfully as he does sparkling, intricate, and severely elaborate pieces, he will take a high rank among the best remembered pianists who have visited this country."[2]

Núñez periodically returned to Puerto Rico. In 1901 he offered a series of concerts in Ponce, Arecibo, San Juan, and Mayagüez.[3] Eight years later he appeared in the Municipal Theatre. The local media of San Juan proudly announced the return of the "eminent Puerto Rican pianist" who had been cheered in Paris, London, Spain, and New York.[4] He appeared in April with several well-known musicians--Julián Andino, Franz Rooms, Manuel Jordán, and María Luisa Lecompte, after which he received a prolonged ovation and high praise from the press.[5]

In the fall of the same year he was featured at a concert at the Ateneo Puertorriqueño in which Manrique de Frierdich with her pupils participated along with "other distinguished artists." The octet of Manuel Tizol played the overture from La Gioconda by Ponchielli. Then, Núñez's Cuarteto de cuerda: Allegro, Tema con variaciones y Final was played by Julián Andino, María Luisa Lecompte, Franz Rooms, and Sergio Lecompte. After a solo, Vorrei by Tosti sung by Encarnita Cestero Mangual accompanied by Manrique de Frierdich, Núñez played Beethoven's Sonata Appasionata. During Part II of the program, a Larghetto for string quartet by Núñez was played and he performed his own piano composition, Sonata Religiosa.[6]

Núñez dedicated his life to the piano and to composition. He performed and was enthusiastically received in Europe, as well as North and South America. Although he left Puerto Rico early in his career, he is known for having interpreted the music of Morel Campos, and he arranged music in Morel Campos' style. Furthermore, some of his music reflected the national mood of the island. An example of this is La Borinqueña, capricho fantástico de la Borinqueña, an arrangement of the national hymn in the form of a fantasía.[7]

A second native who left the island was the internationally famous tenor, Antonio Paoli (1873-1946). Born in Ponce, the son of Domingo and Amalia (Marcano) Paoli, he left at the age of twelve for studies in Spain where he attended concerts by two famous tenors--Julian Gaurré and Francesco Tamagno--and thereby was inspired to embark on an operatic career. He showed such great promise that while in Spain he was granted an annual stipend by the Queen, María Christina de Bourbon. He was graduated from the Real Monasterio del Escorial with an A.B. degree, after which he briefly attended the Toledo Military Academy. Unhappy with military discipline, he entered the Academy of La Scala in Milan in 1897, and two years later came his Paris debut in Grand Opera--in Rossini's William Tell. He appeared in London in 1900[8] and after a triumphant season there he returned to San Juan. He received a cool reception, likely because the opera companies listed him as a Spaniard rather than a native of the island.[9] By 1901, he resolved the problem by returning once more to his homeland, this time as a native son. A public reception was waiting at the wharf to welcome him and his wife back to Puerto Rico.[10] A public meeting in the Plaza was held to demonstrate support for this "renowned son" of their country.

A description of his visit clearly demonstrates the triumphant return of a native son. While in San Juan, he gave a concert in the Municipal Theatre,[11] sang during a Novena in honor of the Virgin Mary in the Church of San José,[12] and performed with the Martínez Casado Dramatic Company. It was reported that the audience was wild with enthusiasm. One reporter wrote: "He is so well known there is no need to mention him here. He sang well, and every note seemed to reach some latent spot in the hearts of his audience."[13] After his final appearance in San Juan in the drama, La Dolores,[14] he left for Arecibo where he was to give two concerts, which had to be postponed because he became ill in the Hotel Italiano.[15] When he recovered he appeared at a sumptuous dance in his honor, and gave a concert, singing operatic arias in costume.[16] Then he went to Ponce, he gave a concert in La Perla Theatre, to a standing room audience. In Ponce, as elsewhere on his tour, he followed the example of Gottschalk, by including the best known musicians of the city on his program.[17] While in Ponce, he sang for a High Mass for the Feast of Corpus Christi, and it was reported to be the most magnificent High Mass ever heard in Ponce.[18]

After brief appearances in Aguidilla,[19] Humacao,[20] and Coamo,[21] he sang a Solemn Mass at the Carmelite Nuns of El Convento in San Juan with Bishop Blenk officiating.[22] His final concert was on July 24, after a three month stay. He sang arias from La Favorita, Rigoletto, Il Trovatore, and La Gioconda, Elisa Tavárez played Silence by Raff and a Chopin Ballade, and Alicia Sicardó played the Nocturne No. 5 by Chopin. When the concert ended, bouquets were thrown and beriboned cloves were sent flying through the air by the delighted audience. Paoli was presented with a magnificent watch from his friend, Don Vicente Balbas, who also was on the program reading poetry.[23]

13

After he left Puerto Rico, he toured the United States singing with the opera company of Mascagni. It was reported that "Señor Paoli has without question the best voice heard in New York this season. It is a pure tenor quality and remarkable for its range. He sings Otello and William Tell in the original key without transposition, a very rare feat indeed."[24]

He also triumphed in Boston and Philadelphia,[25] and in 1903 in Venice, and in 1904 in Moscow and St. Petersburg, where the Czar and Czarina sent an invitation to Paoli to come to their box and the Czar decorated him.[26] He sang in Rome in 1905, where he was proclaimed the best tenor in the world,[27] and had a debut in Madrid singing Verdi's Moor with Celestina Boninsegna as Desdemona.[28] Puerto Rican newspapers followed his travels, and proudly kept the people informed of Paoli's accomplishments.[29] During the 1909-1910 opera season he made his debut at La Scala in Samson et Dalila.

He recorded for La Voce del Padrone (the Italian branch of R.C.A. Victor), took part in a recording of I Pagliacci conducted by Leoncavallo, one of the earliest of such attempts on records. The composer selected Paoli for the role of Canio. The size of his voice and its facility in the highest range dictated resounding success. His voice was overwhelming in its power. When he sang Wagner's Lohengrin at the performance in honor of the emperor in the Viennese Imperial Theatre, which was filled with members of the court and high society, he received a tremendous ovation. The emperor, overcome with emotion, rose to his feet and as a result, the entire audience rose and the great tenor bowed low before a thundering applause.[30] An honorary title was bestowed upon him by Kaiser Wilhelm of Germany and Emperor Franz Joseph of Austria.[31] In 1902, his first wife, Josefina Vestira, died and in 1924 he married an Italian Adelaide Bonini, in Milan; in 1928 they returned to Puerto Rico to make their permanent home. After suffering a stroke in 1932 he was awarded a pension by the Puerto Rico legislature (1934).[32] One of his greatest fans, Jesús López of Vega-Alta, has built a shrine, a small house filled with mementos from Paoli's life.

A third native who left Puerto Rico was Francisco P. Cortés Gonzalo (1873-1950). A native of San Juan, he moved in 1880 to Ponce, where he was a pupil of

Tavárez. He became an extraordinary pianist, far better known in foreign countries than he was in San Juan. At a fiesta organized by Maestro J. O. Pasarell of Ponce, he played during a concert by such well-known musicians as Arístides Chavier, who won first prize. When Cortés finished playing, Tavárez, "el immortal," put his arm around the boy and told the audience that Cortés had only been studying with him for twenty-three months, whereupon Chavier renounced his prize and gave it to the boy.[33]

In 1893, at the age of 20, he went to the Liceo Filharmonico de Barcelona to study under the direction of Professor Vicente Costa Noguerra. In the same year, on June 15, he was awarded first prize in piano and a silver medal in his musical technique, which he had studied with Francisco P. Sánchez at the Conservatorio de Barcelona.[34] Winning that prize made it possible for him to receive a modest stipend from the Provincial Governor of Puerto Rico to pursue studies in Paris. In 1895, he was named professor of piano at the Joan of Arc College in Paris. He received a certificate for his studies with Theodore Dubois in 1896, and graduated from the Paris Conservatoire in 1897. In 1900 he organized the orchestra of the Galería Georges Petit which played the opening concert at the Grand International Exposition. He was a member of the music committee and his group also played a concert in honor of the foreign delegation.[35] He remained in France until 1906 as an orchestral director at the Casino of Houlgate. He was decorated by the French Government, and the Ministry of Public Education and Fine Arts conferred the praise of the French Academy on him. He was the only Puerto Rican to receive this high honor.[36]

He returned to Puerto Rico by way of New York and in December directed a performance of his work, Nuit de Noel featuring Amalia Paoli. For this work, which had also been performed in Paris, he wrote a screen play for the movies, titled Fortune Teller of Seville.[37]

In 1907, when he returned to Puerto Rico, he was greeted by Manuel Fernández Juncos, president of the Society of Writers and Artists. Cortés presented three concerts in the Municipal Theatre.[38] Later in February he gave a concert in La Perla Theatre and in March he was the maestro director and composer at a "gran festival" featuring Amalia Paoli.[39] In April, he participated in concerts with other distinguished Puerto Rican artists.[40]

He lamented the lack of a good conservatory of music in Puerto Rico and suggested to the authorities that one be created at the University.[41] He left on May first for Paris via New York on the ship Caracas.[42] He later settled in New York where he taught at the Malquin School of Music and during the next ten years was the director of the orchestras of the Hotel Vanderbilt, the Waldorf Astoria, and at Delmonico's Restaurant. He also taught in a private school.[43]

These performers' long absences in foreign countries also contributed to the idea that there was a void in their country's culture, even though they visited periodically. They were outstanding musicians but each was better known in other countries. These are the last of the Puerto Rican students to study in Europe at government expense. The government of Puerto Rico had previously granted scholarships to students to study abroad. During the Spanish rule, Puerto Rican musicians had the opportunity to study with European musicians and gained experience abroad before returning to their native land. With the change of government, this practice was discontinued, and this is another reason for the feeling of cultural decline.

The Church had been the principal patron of the island's arts, and with the separation of church and state, resulting from American control, the Church was unable to support its musicians. During the Spanish regime there were small orchestras in the churches in Puerto Rico. Under the patronage of the Church, composers had the opportunity to have their works performed during the church services. The instrumentation included strings, woodwinds, and brass, and ensembles represented the Romantic Period of operatic influence, especially that of Italy in the nineteenth century. There were three especially fine orchestras in Old San Juan: the orchestra of the Cathedral directed by Felip Gutiérrez, an orchestra in the Church of San José established by the Jesuits and directed by Gregorio Ledesma, composition teacher and organist, and the orchestra of the parish of San Francisco, directed by Sandalio Callejo.[44]

16

When the United States took control of the island, church property was used for military purposes and troops occupied the buildings. In Old San Juan, the land extending to the sea wall had belonged to the church since Ponce de León, the conqueror and first governor, donated it to the Dominican Friars for a monastery. The monastery, renamed by the United States and occupied by troops, was called Barracks of Santo Domingo and the Ballajá Barracks.[45] All state subsidies to the church ceased. Church property titles were held in Spain, and the municipal governments of Puerto Rico were ready to take over title to the Catholic Churches, convents, monasteries, rectories, and cemetaries. Suddenly, the Church was in critical financial condition because of the loss of title to its property. In addition, public charities were controlled by the Church, and the removal of government aid caused a social welfare crisis.[46]

The Spanish influence in Puerto Rico dates back over four hundred years, and Puerto Rico is essentially an old world country. Styles and dress came from Spain and France before the Spanish-American War and the cultural heritage was Spanish. A final reason for the feeling that a cultural regression took place was that it was quite difficult to do business with men who did not speak Spanish.[47] Most of the men appointed to fill executive positions in Puerto Rico came from the United States with no knowledge of Spanish, and little understanding of Spanish culture or temperament. Theodore Roosevelt was the first governor who learned the language well enough to dispense with an interpreter, and he made his speeches in Spanish. His predecessors had told him to make the Puerto Ricans speak English to him.[48] Roosevelt felt that this was mere laziness on their part, and he delighted in the fact that he could converse with the natives.[49] The new American leaders tried to substitute English for Spanish, and the Puerto Rican people felt that they were being asked to abandon their ancestral tongue. Related to this was the fact that the Americans refused to authorize holidays on the traditional feast days.[50]

Although there was not a cultural regression at this time, the Puerto Ricans did experience an economic regression throughout the island. When the United States changed from the silver to the gold

17

standard in 1898, it caused a depression in Puerto Rico. Commodities increased in value fifty percent, and the sudden rise in prices resulted in economic chaos.

The Puerto Rican peso was quoted lower than the Mexican peso, worth about 37 cents.[51] This was a handicap. The reduced exchange rate paralyzed trade with the United States, and English ships which formerly stopped in Puerto Rico no longer did so because of the lack of cargo.

When the civil government assumed control, with the inauguration of Governor Charles H. Allen, on May 1, 1900, the retirement of the Spanish and Puerto Rican currency was also begun.[52] By 1903 only American currency circulated.[53] The United States did not replace Spain as a buyer of Puerto Rican products. This caused a critical situation. Spain ceased buying Puerto Rican coffee. Marketable products went unwanted and, as a result, farmers had no money to hire labor, so there was no one to pick the products or to handle them after they were picked. Puerto Rico needed the American market, and needed the food products from the north.

Unfortunately, Puerto Rican coffee was too strong for the Americans. In October of 1903, The San Juan News printed a huge advertisement informing people how to prepare their coffee to make it more palatable to Americans.[54] Spain was far away and unable to absorb the quantities of products such as tobacco and sugar produced in Puerto Rico. Therefore, the small farmer was literally forced back into the hills.

Puerto Rico was not a self sufficient island before the invasion. It imported most of its food from abroad, principally from the United States. But now, in order to have fair trade between the United States and Puerto Rico, there were many obstacles to overcome, such as American tariffs.

By this time, most of the islanders felt that their homeland was as bad off commercially as it had been before 1812. "The economic situation was not quite bright . . . . Free trade had ended, the coffee producers were hard hit because their chief markets, Spain and Cuba were now lost to them."[55] Many Puerto Ricans left for other Spanish speaking countries. According to The San Juan News, several prominent Puerto Rican residents left in May of 1902 on the Steamer Ciudad de Cadiz, to take up permanent residence in Spain.[56]

To add to the problems, on August 8, 1899, the hurricane of San Ciriaco devastated the island.[57] Up to this time, twenty-one hurricanes had hit Puerto Rico from November 16, 1492 until 1899. To that date this was the worst recorded storm. Although it had been predicted for seven days, it swept through Guadalupe, Jamaica, Cuba, Saint Thomas, and Puerto Rico bringing death and destruction. It left houses, churches, hospitals, schools, and theatres destroyed. In Old San Juan, balconies were ripped off the houses along Cristo Street, the cavalry barracks were destroyed, storehouses and other public buildings were partially demolished, and hundreds of native houses were wrecked.[58] At the other end of the island in Mayagüez most of the houses were in ruins.[59] In Río Piedras, the Catholic Church, the cemetary and schools were destroyed, and in Humacao the Hotel Victoria was completely destroyed.[60] After the hurricane there was widespread suffering. Farmers in the interior were starving. Their coffee plantations, cattle, property and crops were destroyed and thousands of laborers were out of work. By August, the death toll had risen to 2500 with another 2000 still missing and about 1000 injured.[61]

The economic crisis continued through the next year. Poverty was widespread and hunger, almost to the point of starvation, was common. In 1901 cases of death from starvation were still noted. A letter of despair was sent by the people to Governor Allen stating that the situation was becoming altogether unbearable.[62]

In 1903 there was still widespread suffering. The economic situation was the main problem. A Puerto Rican law student in his senior year at Cornell University, Martín Travieso, Jr., wrote an editorial for The San Juan News, stating that

"Conditions in Puerto Rico are far worse than they were under the rule of Spain, and that the government party is carrying on with a high hand, favoring a minority which consists of worthless politicians, while the best and honest people suffer . . . . Governor Hunt lives luxuriously in a place

far more magnificent than the White House
and his retinue is elaborate, while the land
around is prostrate.

To gain his point he allies himself with
the minority party, which consists of
American adventurers and native
renegades."[63]

The economic crisis experienced on the island
affected the people in nearly all phases of their
existence. The separation of church and state left
the churches in poverty. The attempt at a change of
language, the newly-imposed customs, the exchange of
currency, the lack of a market for farm products, and
the worst hurricane in centuries all took their toll
and promoted feelings of insecurity among the people.
It is little wonder that everyone expected a cultural
regression.

NOTES

1. Arístides Chavier Arévalo. "Gonzalo Núñez," La Democracia, (November 10, 1915), in the Archivo General de Puerto Rico Reference Room, Vol. 3, p. 52. See also Colección Monserrate Deliz (CP 31, Box 7, No. 124h) in the Archivo General.

2. The New York Times, (December 12, 1877), 5. The compositions he selected were later to become popular repertoire among Puerto Rico pianists--Chopin Andante Spianato, Polonaise, and Rondo, a Mozart Allegro, and a Bach Fugue.

3. Compositores Puertorriqueños, p. 7, and María Luisa Muñoz, La música . . . , p. 124.

4. BM, LXXI/70 (March 29, 1909), 2.

5. Ibid., LXXI/80 (April 10, 1909), 2; LXXI/81 (April 12, 1909), 2; LXXI/84 (April 15, 1909), 2, and LXXI/86 (April 17, 1909), 2.

6. Ibid., LXXI/221 (September 11, 1909), 1. He returned to the island August 24, according to La Correspondencia de Puerto Rico [from now on abbreviated LaC], (August 25, 1909), 5, and (October 21, 1909), 1. Also see BM, LXXI/238 (October 1, 1909), 1.

7. A manuscript copy of his La Borinqueña, capricho fantástico de La Borinqueña and many other pieces for piano including El Angelus, Argonessa, Doux songs, dedicated to Braulio Dueño Colón, Fleur de Lis (vals), (Augener Co., 1904), Hélène (vals brillante), Lorelay, Las dos palomas (danza Cubana), La Mariposa,(capricho para piano, Op. 2), and Recuerdos da Andalucía (bolero para piano). Works not in the Archivo General but listed in the Colección Monserrate Deliz (CP 31, mentioned above), include an Allegro de Concierto, Gavota, Trina, Mazurka, and a danza criolla de concierto, Una Noche en Puerto Rico.

8. According to Max de Schauensee in "The Lion of Ponce, "Opera News, XXXVI/20 (April 8, 1972), 6-7, Paoli never sang at the Metropolitan Opera House nor at Covent Garden, but Alahija L. Cortijo in La música popular y los músicos celebres de la América Latina. Barcelona: Casa Editorial Maucci, 1903, p. 429, places Paoli in Covent Garden in 1900, as does the editorial, "Antonio Paoli, breves datos biografícos," Nosotros, I/14 (March-April, 1966), 11.

9. Helen V. Tooker, "Puerto Rico's Tenor," San Juan Review, III/3 (April, 1966), 4.

10. The San Juan News [from now on abbreviated SJN], VI/108 (May 9, 1901), 8, and VI/109 (May 10, 1901), 8.

11. BM, LXIII/109 (May 11, 1901), 1, and a rave review in LXIII/110 (May 13, 1901), 1.

12. Ibid., LXIII/111 (May 14, 1901), 1.

13. SJN, VI/111 (May 14, 1901), 8.

14. Ibid., p. 8, and VI/115 (May 17, 1901), 1.

15. Ibid., p. 8.

16. BM, LXIII/118 (May 22, 1901), 1, and SJN, VI/123 (May 25, 1901), 3.

17. SJN, VI/126 (May 30, 1901), 3; VI/127 (June 1, 1901), 3; VI/114 (May 16, 1901), 3; VI/127 (June 1, 1901), 3, and VI/130 (June 5, 1901), 5.

18. Ibid., VI/133 (June 8, 1901), 3.

19. BM, LXIII/136 (June 11, 1901), 3.

20. SJN, VI/137 (June 13, 1901), 5.

21. Ibid., VI/150 (June 29, 1901), 3; La Democracia, XI/2927 (July 3, 1901), 1.

22. SJN, VI/163 (July 17, 1901), 3.

23. Ibid., VI/169 (July 24, 1901), 5; VI/170 (July 25, 1901), 5.

24. "Señor Antonio Paoli," The Puerto Rico Herald, I/44 (May 10, 1902), 6, and Ibid., I/41 (April 19, 1902), 8-9. Helen V. Tooker, p. 4, places Paoli in New York in 1901. The BM, LXIV/108 (May 10, 1902), 1, quoted the North American Press release from the Commercial Advertiser which stated that his voice was clear, flowing, and vibrant but pure. He was received enthusiastically.

25. The Puerto Rico Herald, I/41 (April 19, 1902), 8-9.

26. Tooker, p. 6.

27. Ibid.

28. Puerto Rico Musical, Revista de Música, (ed. by Arteaga), I/1 (February 15, 1906, 11. He triumphed in Madrid.

According to LaC, XVI (January 27, 1906), 1, his debut was in Otello and Il Trovatore.

29. BM, LXVIII/204 (August 30, 1906), 2; LaC, XVII (March 25, 1907), 2; "El Gran Tenor Puertorriqueño: Antonio Paoli: una escritura por valor de 250,000 francos," El Carnaval, IX/17 [San Juan] (March 29, 1908), 16; and "Hispanoamericanos Ilustres," Espiritisimo, III/36 (April, 1969), 1.

30. Tooker, p. 6.

31. Ibid.

32. Ibid., and a printed program dated February 28, 1936, in Elisa Tavárez's Scrapbook 1933 (Colección Elisa Tavárez CP 9, No. 1) shows that the title Teatro Antonio Paoli was used for the Municipal Theatre but a later legislative assembly transferred the honor to Alejandro Tapia.

33. Arístides Chavier, "Está aquí el gran pianista don Francisco P. Cortés," El Mundo, (November 8, 1937), 15. Archivo General de Puerto Rico Reference Room Vol. IX.

34. "Francisco P. Cortés," The Puerto Rico Herald, I/14 (October 12, 1901), 6.

35. Chavier, El Mundo, p. 15.

36. Ibid., p. 17.

37. BM, LXIV/261 (November 11, 1906), 3, Cortés, who occupied an honorable post in that French city, sent a two-step he had composed for one of the municipal bands in San Juan. Ibid., LXVIII/290 (December 8, 1906), 1, notes that he arrived in San Juan, and ibid., LXVIII/300 (December 20, 1906), 7, lists the performances.

38. Ibid., LXIX/4 (January 5, 1907), 4; LXIX/11 (January 14, 1907), 2; LXIX/16 (January 19, 1907), 2; LXIX/17 (January 21. 1907), 2; LXIX/21 (January 25, 1907), 2; LXIX/22 (January 26, 1907), 7; LaC, XVII (January 14, 1907), 4; XVII (January 21, 1907), 1, 2; XVII (January 28, 1907), 1, 2.

39. BM, LXIX/47 (February 25, 1907), 5.

40. Ibid., LXIX/72 (March 26, 1907), 4; LXIX/82 (April 8, 1907), 2, and LXIX/99 (April 27, 1907), 2; LaC, XVII (March 14, 1907), 4, and (March 25, 1907), 3; XVII (April 16, 1907), 2, and (April 29, 1907), 2.

41. Ibid., and BM, LXIX/99 (April 27, 1907), 2.

42. Chavier, El Mundo, p. 15.

43. LaC, XVII (May 1, 1907), 2, and Chavier, El Mundo, p. 7.

44. José Antonio Daubón. Cosas de Puerto Rico, II. San Juan:
    Tip. La Correspondencia, 1904-5, p. 57. Daubón states that
    the orchestra was created by Fray Benigno Carrión de Málaga.
    According to Emilio J. Pasarell, Esculcando el Siglo XIX en
    Puerto Rico. Barcelona: Rumbos, 1967, pp. 31-32, the
    orchestra of the cathedral was organized September 9, 1858
    by Gutiérrez, director of the capilla. It had the following
    members: Miguel Herrera, organist, Claudio Grandy and
    Aniceto Andino, Violins 1 and 2, Francisco Martínez, Violin
    3, Salvador Ramos, Clarinet 1, Vicente Franco, Clarinet 2,
    Francisco Borrás, Trumpet 1, Juan Noriega, Trumpet 2,
    Eduardo Martorell, Flute, Juan Bastar, Ophicleide, Manuel
    Martínez, Cello, Aurelio Dueño, Contralto, José Salavent,
    Tenor 1, José Benevent, Tenor 2, Tiburcio Portillo, bass.

45. United States House of Representatives Documents No. 5557,
    60th Congress, 2nd Session, Document No. 1204, pp. 7-8.

46. BM, LXIII/237 (October 15, 1901), 4, printed the following
    story of one couple's hardship. When they went to the priest
    to be married, he told them, no money, no marriage. The
    woman set out to find the money and when she returned with
    it, he married them. "Anything on your mind?" he asked.
    "Well I would like to know if anything could spoil our
    marriage?" "Certainly not," he said, "I have nothing more to
    do with your marriage." "That eases my mind," she said. "And
    God bless you, Reverend. There's the ticket for your hat. I
    picked it up in the hallway and pawned it."

47. A. Liebes, "Puerto Rico Not Prospering Under the United
    States Rule," reprinted from The New York Times, (October 4,
    1903), in The Puerto Rico Herald, III/115 (October 10,
    1903), 979-980.

48. Theodore Roosevelt. Colonial Policies of the United States.
    New York: Arno Press and the New York Times, 1970, p. 100.

49. Ibid.

50. Brau, p. 81.

51. SJN, I/1 (November 9, 1899), 2.

52. Ibid., VII/100 (May 1, 1900), 1.

53. Ibid., VIII/219 (September 25, 1903), 5.

54. Ibid., VIII/237 (October 16, 1903), 5.

55. María Teresa Babín. La cultura de Puerto Rico. San Juan: Instituto de Cultura Puertorriqueña, 1970, p. 93.

56. SJN, VIII/219 (September 25, 1903), 5.

57. Paul Nelson Chiles. The Puerto Rican Press Reactions to the United States, 1888-1898. Philadelphia: University of Pennsylvania Press, 1944, p. 50.

58. See Ramón Araez y Ferrando. Historia del ciclón del Día de San Ciriaco. San Juan: Imp. Heraldo Español, 1905, p. 7. They were still celebrating the anniversary of the hurricane in 1905: BM, LXVII/179 (August 8, 1905), 1, carried the story of the two memorable days in Puerto Rican history, August 8 and July 25th; and The New York Times, XLVIII (August 10, 1899), 1.

59. Ibid.

60. Ibid., pp. 30, 43.

61. Ibid., pp. 223 and 227, and 48 (August 22, 1899), 6.

62. The Puerto Rico Herald, I/4 (August 31, 1901), 10.

63. Ibid., III/115 (October 10, 1903), 3, (p. 979). According to the SJN, VIII/7 (January 10, 1903), 8. When he returned to San Juan after his graduation from Cornell, Travieso became a well-known lawyer and leading citizen.

GENERAL BROOKE'S EXPEDITION LANDING AT ARROYO IN 1898

Chapter III

THE ARRIVAL OF THE AMERICANS

The American troops landed on the southern end of the island on July 25, 1898, and on October 18, military control passed from Spain to the United States and the command of the troops was transferred to Major General John R. Brooke, United States Army, who had also been in charge of the evacuation commission and who by virtue of this assignment became the military governor of Puerto Rico.

Brooke retained the local Puerto Rican cabinet. On December 9th, Brooke was appointed Military Governor of Cuba and Commander of the Division of Cuba and he was succeeded in Puerto Rico by General Guy B. Henry. Henry dissolved the cabinet and established new government departments, (including an Executive Council, an upper house of the legislature, with five Puerto Ricans and six Americans who were also heads of government departments.) All were appointed by the President with the approval of the United States Senate. The lower house consisted of thirty-five Puerto Ricans chosen in a general election and a resident commissioner who sat in Congress but had no vote. The President also appointed the higher judges. Each department was responsible to the corresponding department in the United States government.[1]

In April of 1899, a new Republican Party was founded in Puerto Rico by Luis Muñoz Rivera, with a pledge of support for the United States:

> "We congratulate ourselves and our country on being under the protection of the American flag, the recognized emblem of Liberty, and will make every effort to advance civilization, to teach loyalty, to love American institutions, and honor Washington, Lincoln, and McKinley, whose names are household words in the land."[2]

Activities on the island appeared to be gradually settling down by April, 1899. A commission headed by Dr. Julio Henna and M. Zeno Gandía presented a petition to President McKinley, requesting that military control over the island be withdrawn and that matters relating to civil government be turned

27

over to the appropriate department in Washington for jurisdiction. It also requested that troops on the island be reduced to a minimum for guarding forts and military posts and that Puerto Ricans be granted a territorial form of government similar to the District of Columbia where citizens had all privileges of United States citizens.[3]

By June, the military presence was reduced, and that adversely affected the local economy. Merchants had sold liberally to the army, and to individual soldiers. In the smaller towns under Spanish rule never had there been so much money in circulation. This was devastating in Arecibo, Yauco, Bayamón, Coamo, and Río Piedras. In San Juan, Ponce, and Mayagüez it was greatly diminished by the reduction of the garrison.

By this time the American sugar companies had grown and prospered more than those owned by the Puerto Ricans because of their business efficiency and sufficient capital. These companies had brought wealth to the island, provided more jobs, and created better working conditions.[4] The impact was so dramatic, The San Juan News predicted that the island would attract a large number of immigrants in the fall of 1899.[5]

Almost from the arrival of the first soldiers, many Puerto Ricans were pleased to escape Spanish control. A tribute appeared in The San Juan News in January, 1900:[6]

WELCOME OF PUERTO RICO
TO THE "YANKEES" ON FIRST LANDING

"So ye have come at last Boys,
While we have waited long,
But we'll forget the past, Boys,
And welcome with a song.
The banner that shall float, Boys,
On summer coasts along,
O'er many a noble boat, Boys,
To quell a mighty wrong.

You are truly welcome, Boys,
A million hearts are glad,
Though still there may be some, Boys,
That take it rather sad.
And yet another few, Boys,

28

Whose patriot souls are mad,
You're welcome to the true, Boys,
And may despise the bad!

Then take a hold that's firm, Boys,
And keep us safe and fast,
Nor heed your German horns, Boys,
That's but an empty blast.
For might is always right, Boys,
When freedom makes a cast;
While though you're long delayed, Boys,
You're welcome here at last !"

The first American Ball held in Puerto Rico was given at the theatre in January, with the entire Eleventh Infantry Band playing the music.[7] Later that month, on the Three Kings Day, there was "masking, serenading, and dancing with lots of music. Every little house was making 'merry' with a dance."[8] By the 16th of January the first American school was erected in Puerto Rico. The flag "fluttered" in the breeze. Puerto Rican children recited the Pledge of Allegiance, and all sang the Star Spangled Banner and Columbia the Gem of the Ocean. There were 350 pupils, 8 teachers, and 1 principal.[9]

Prior to this period, the Archbishop of New Orleans, Plácido Luis Chapelle, was appointed Apostolic Delegate to oversee Cuba, the Philippines, and Puerto Rico. Finally, in April, 1899, Monsignor Jaime Huberto Blenk was appointed Bishop of Puerto Rico.[10] He had been Rector of the College of the Marist Fathers in New Orleans, and the Auditor and Secretary to Archbishop Chapelle. By July, the Bishop arrived in Puerto Rico.[11] According to all reports, he spent a great deal of time among the people. Almost immediately he distributed food to the poor.[12] The following spring The San Juan News declared that he was a good, faithful prelate, a trustworthy advisor, constantly among his people and thoroughly aware of their needs.[13] An example of his work can be seen from his visit to Lares; he was the first Bishop to come there in twelve years! A large mounted escort of prominent citizens greeted him and under a handsome embroidered canopy carried by six men, escorted him to the Church. There he confirmed between 1500 and 2000 children.[14] The Puerto Ricans gave him a large reception that summer in Santa Ana Church following the services. Francisco

Verar directed the orchestra for the affair, and Teresina Calderón, Aguayo Orbeta, and Cecilia Bruno all sang.[15]

Bishop Blenk participated in civic affairs such as the inauguration of the governor on July 4, 1904. After the band played Hail to the Chief, he led the prayer.[16] News items usually referred to him as the "illustrious" Bishop and as early as October, 1905, it was rumored that he would become Archbishop of New Orleans; by February of 1906 he received that appointment.[17]

While in Puerto Rico, the Bishop wrote many pleas to the United States Congress and to President Theodore Roosevelt concerning the confiscated properties of the Church. He received many promises but no action. In dispute were the Barracks of Santo Domingo, valued at $100,710, the Ballajá Barracks, valued at $182,110, the site of the city market place, valued at $11,000, the chapel of the Boy's Charity School, valued at $1,093, the site of the insane asylum, valued at $128,112, the San Francisco Barracks, valued at $158,818, and a tract of about sixty acres of grazing land near San Juan. The Church also claimed certain "censos" held by the treasurer of Puerto Rico, liens on real estate granted from time to time by individuals to the Church, amounting to about $120,000.[18] Finally, the Supreme Court held that ownership of such property in Ponce had resided with and would remain in the Church.[19] In 1908, Congress appropriated $120,000 to the Bishop of Puerto Rico for the use of the buildings and land owned by the Church.[20]

Assistance was given fairly consistently to the people of the island. In May of 1900, Governor Henry had been replaced by Governor-General George W. Davis, and the wife of the former Governor organized a Colonial Aid Society and issued an urgent appeal for help for the inhabitants of the island. Through The New York Times, Mrs. Henry asked for clothing, medicine, and money.[21] Governor Henry repeated her request in July, when he addressed the New York Merchants Association and described conditions in Puerto Rico and explained the problems.[22] He stated that the greatest need was education and for the Puerto Ricans to have an opportunity to help themselves. They wanted to become Americans, he said, but they did not want to become Americanized. They were willing to be governed by the laws of the United States, he went on, but did not want to be over-run by "Carpet-baggers." The Puerto Ricans were looking to the United States for the means of improving their conditions. The appeal by the Henrys obviously was heard; they received substantial gifts from the Merchants Society, as well as from individuals, including J. Pierpont Morgan and John Wanamaker.[23] Major General George W. Davis and his wife, who was of Spanish ancestry, also worked hard to relieve conditions of the poor and all those who were affected by the hurricane. Mrs. Davis was active in the Ladies Aid Society and donated considerable sums to local hospitals and other charitable institutions.[24]

After the Hurricane of San Ciriaco in August of 1899, an appeal to the American people was published in various American newspapers. It was reported that Ponce was devastated as was its port, damage to which was estimated at $250,000.[25] It was estimated that about 2000 persons drowned in the Ponce district alone.[26] Villages were swept out of existence. Along with the commercial depression, the calamity brought terrible conditions to Puerto Rico.[27] Secretary of War Elihu Root made an appeal to the American Governors for relief.[28] The army transport "McPherson" sailed with a cargo of supplies and donations from merchants associations, especially from Boston and New York City.[29]

Again, Mrs. Henry's Colonial Aid Society appealed to the American people through an announcement carried by the Associated Press.[30] The Acting Mayor of New York issued an appeal, and responses came quickly from the merchants and bankers.[31] In Boston the Puerto Rico relief fund reached $10,065; the Mayor of Baltimore expected to raise $15,000 but he refused to send supplies on the same ship as the city of Philadelphia. He asked the government to provide a ship.[32] Thousands of articles of clothing were sent on the Steamship "Evelyn"[33] and funds continued to pour in, including donations from President William McKinley and John D. Rockefeller.[34] A total of $89,754 was raised in the United States,[35] and tons of supplies were transported to the island.[36] The United States Congress also sent $200,000 in food and materials.[37]

By 1900 in Puerto Rico, the wives of the Army and

Navy officers had organized the Ladies Aid Society of San Juan to do sewing for the poor.[38] The organization was quite active and sponsored many benefit programs.

The newspapers in Jamaica drew a significant parallel between the American and English methods of meeting colonial emergencies. The papers cynically observed that while England was about to raise funds to assist the Leeward Islands, the Americans had already dispatched supplies to Puerto Rico.[39] In Cuba, however, an editorial in El Diario de la marina noted that prior to the American take-over, Puerto Rico was the most prosperous island in the West Indies:

"Now all is changed and seriously disturbed by the radical and sudden modifications of local customs. Puerto Rico is refused a political organization by her new masters. She is not allowed even the autonomy that existed under the old regime. The cyclone that has devastated the island is a symbol of that just wrath of God toward the American occupation."[40]

Missionaries from the United States who visited also reported that education problems abounded. In October of 1899, Reverend W. H. Ward reported to the American Missionary Association on the educational and religious conditions prevailing on the island. Ward said that "the school system of Puerto Rico is as bad as it well can be. There is . . . a college which gives a degree of A.B. and which takes a boy perhaps into the freshman year of college."[41] He further stated that the man who was in charge of the island's educational system had installed his daughter as head of the normal school, his son-in-law as president of the college, and six other relatives in positions of importance. Ward observed that in rural areas, the teachers took their pupils into their homes, reserving two rooms for classes of thirty to fifty pupils. The men taught the boys and the women, the girls. Students had no books and were required to pay a fee if they could afford to. He also noted that the Puerto Ricans did not go to Church nor did they have any respect for their priests. He quoted Father Sherman, son of General William Sherman, as having said that Puerto Rico is a "Catholic country without religion."[42] In a letter to a Catholic newspaper, Father Sherman had explained that the reason for this condition was largely political--the priests were supported by the Spanish government and were regarded as spies and emissaries of that government.

With the American control, schools in Puerto Rico were modeled after those in the United States, and when possible, Puerto Rican children were sent to study on the mainland. In a message to the Legislative Assembly (January, 1903) regarding the educational system of the island, the Governor stated that "Since the institution of civil government, there has been steady progress in education, and the record of the past year is very gratifying."[43] He noted that in three years, the number of schools had almost doubled (682-1100), and the number of students similarly improved (30,000 to 55,000). He stated that forty-five young people had been sent to the United States at an annual cost of $15,000, and that in Puerto Rico there were Boys' and Girls' Charity Schools, a system of industrial training modeled after similar institutions in the United States.

By April of 1903 reporters boasted in the newspapers that school facilties had been increased, roads had been enlarged, new agricultural regions had opened up, and some New Yorkers had opened a sugar mill at an expenditure of $3,000,000, with natives holding most of the jobs.[44]

In September of 1903, an article on the "Brilliant Future of Puerto Rico" cited the Department of Health's latest report that there were 13,000 fewer deaths this year on the island than in the previous year.[45] It also stated that formerly much of the money raised by taxation had gone to Spain, but now, for the first time, money raised by taxation remained on the island. The article also stated that the "thinking men" of the island realized that the United States administration has been generous to them, allowing them to keep and use certain house receipts and internal revenue. The article closed with the remark that "the people look forward to statehood."

There were many changes between 1898 and 1903. Tobacco and sugar had replaced coffee as the main product in Puerto Rico, and there were material changes such as the introduction of trolley-cars, telegraph, telephones, and electricity. In addition, the "new" game of baseball was increasing in popularity.

With American control, the bands added marches by Sousa to their repertoire, and when the former street urchins were enrolled in the girls' and boys' charity schools in Santurce, there was a first-rate band composed entirely of students.

Yet, although Puerto Ricans appeared to appreciate the wealth and reforms brought by the Americans, there clearly was another side of the story.[46] For instance, when Theodore Roosevelt arrived in 1906 for a one-day visit on his homeward-bound trip from Panama, the Boletín Mercantil de Puerto Rico reported that the townspeople would all congregate, there would be music and great rejoicing and as he would pass from one end of the island to the other, people would welcome him everywhere. Yet, by travelling on the military road, the President

> "will, perhaps, believe that all the roads on the island are on a par with this one and in a similar state of preservation. And as he journeys through the towns on route he will see the children of the public schools drawn up conspicuously for his inspection; the children who are unable to go to school, because they are without clothes, will not be in evidence.
>
> And during the few hours of his soujourn in San Juan, surrounded always by the bureaucracy and feted by everyone, the First Magistrate of the Nation will not be able to grasp the real necessities and needs of the country; he will not be able to hear even one of the many complaints which the stupidity and selfishness of the present regime have made necessary . . . . It would only be necessary for him to see with his own eyes those things which others have not wished to see, things that the congregantes have endeavored to conceal, for him, to usher in the hour of justice, and the colony would smile with happiness thinking that the plots and schemes of the bureaucrats, who aimed to convert the island into a feudalism, had been frustrated."[47]

34

The first editorial that followed the visit was one of hope for the country. This was the dividing time between American colonization as it was and as it would be in the future. The second editorial mentioned the President's brief trip across the island, the presence of extraordinary number of school children and the fact that the President commented on this. However, it pointed out that he did not see the 300,000 children who could not attend school because the funds for education had already been used. Because the government did not have sufficient funds for all of the children to attend school, the editor declared

"It seems only fair and just that the national government should contribute an amount sufficient for the erection of new schools in the Island.

Such an act would, in a measure, indemnify us for the injury and damage sustained by the operation of the so-called free trade imposed upon us by the present regime, a free trade which does not protect our coffee in the way that all products of the United States are protected here.

The spectacle offered by the thousands of creatures condemned to want and ignorance by an injustice of this sort is painful to contemplate; it is pitiful to realize that in spite of the knowledge of the misfortune of these neglected creatures, we are powerless to improve their miserable condition for lack of the resources that would make it possible.

A splendid remembrance of the visit of President Roosevelt to Puerto Rico would be for all the children of the Island to be able to attend school."[48]

When Theodore Roosevelt returned to the United States, he documented his Puerto Rican observations in a message to the Congress.[49] He noted that in every town there was a gathering of school children. He observed that the main emphasis was placed on the primary grades and that every effort was being made to secure the benefits of elementary education to all Puerto Ricans of the next generation and to train them so that the industrial, agricultural, and commercial opportunities of the island would be utilized to the best possible advantage. As he traveled around the island he noted the rapid growth in the fruit industry as well as in sugar cane and tobacco. He told the Congress that the previous year (1906) was the most prosperous one that the island had ever known, either before or since the American occupation. He praised the people of Puerto Rico, stating that they were loyal to the American flag, and he urged Congress to grant them full citizenship.[50]

In the Governor's Report to the Congress, Winthrop stated that economic conditions were greatly improved and the production of sugar, tobacco, and coffee had increased.[51] There was a more liberal system of government and a more equitable method of conducting elections; because of the improved economic conditions there was an increase in deposits and earnings in the various banks. These improved conditions provided a great amount of work for laborers. There was also an attempt to improve the livestock on the island. Livestock was introduced from the United States for the purpose of improving the bread of domestic animals. The animals were placed in charge of the director of the agricultural school of the University of Puerto Rico at Río Piedras.[52]

Soon after the reports were read, a debate developed on Puerto Rican citizenship: The Puerto Ricans had been citizens of Spain and now that they had been deprived of the citizenship, they felt that they had been "subjected to the greatest abuse to which cultured men could be called upon to endure in a civilized and democratic age."[53] The President should have been able to awaken in the Congress a spirit of justice, but this did not occur. Puerto Rico was again to be an "abandoned" island.

NOTES

1. By 1909 this was deemed inefficient and the island was placed under the Bureau of Insular Affairs in the War Department. This form of government continued until 1917, when the Puerto Ricans were made citizens of the United States.

2. The New York Times, XLVIII (April 1, 1899), 8. Luis Muñoz Rivera had been a leader of the extinct Federal Party and moved to New York when he was editor of the weekly newspaper, The Puerto Rico Herald.

3. Ibid., Henna had been active in the revolutionary movement against Spain back in 1868-69 and was expatriated by the Spanish in 1869. He studied medicine at Columbia University and remained a loyal Puerto Rican. See The Puerto Rico Herald, I/4 (August 3, 1901), 2-3.

4. The New York Times, XLVIII (June 14, 1899), 9.

5. SJN, III/146 (October 12, 1899), 2.

6. Ibid., IV/9 (January 7, 1900), 5.

7. Ibid., IV/7 (January 6, 1900), 1.

8. Ibid., IV/21 (January 14, 1900), 1.

9. Ibid., IV/23 (January 16, 1900), 1.

10. BM, LXI/95 (April 22, 1899), 1.

11. El País, V/164 (July 14, 1899), 2.

12. SJN, V/49 (August 28, 1900), 1.

13. Ibid., VI/57 (March 8, 1901), 4.

14. Ibid., VI/127 (June 1, 1901), 3.

15. Ibid., VII/273 (August 9, 1902), 4, and VII/274 (August 10, 1902), 8.

16. Ibid., IX/150 (June 30, 1904), 5.

17. The Puerto Rico Eagle, IV (October 17, 1905), 8, and BM, LXVIII/43 (February 20, 1906), 2.

18. United States Senate Document 5393, 60th Congress, 2nd

Session, Document No. 578. Annual Report of the Governor of Puerto Rico, June 30, 1908 (Washington, D.C.: Government Printing Office, 1909), p. 18; According to SJN, IX/241 (October 15, 1904), 3, Secretary Charles Hartzell also filed suit for Puerto Rico, as did Atty. Juan Hernández López in 1905 (The Puerto Rico Eagle, IV (October 13, 1905), 8.

19. United States House of Representatives Document No. 5557, 60th Congress, 2nd Session, Document No. 1204, p. 3.

20. For a complete report see United States Report No. 2977, 57th Congress, 2nd Session. Transcript of Record. Supreme Court of the United States October Term, 1908. Document No. 151. Also see Decision of the Supreme Court of Porto Rico and the Dissenting Opinion in the Case of the Roman Catholic Apostolic Church of Porto Rico vs. the People of Porto Rico (Washington, D.C.: Government Printing Office, 1909).

21. The New York Times, XLVIII (July 9, 1899), 18.

22. Ibid., (July 19, 1899), 12.

23. Ibid.

24. SJN, IX/190 (August 18, 1904), 1.

25. The New York Times, XLVIII (August 11, 1899), 1.

26. Ibid., (August 13, 1899), 2.

27. Ibid.

28. Ibid., (August 15, 1899), 4.

29. Ibid.

30. Ibid., (August 13, 1899), 4.

31. Ibid.

32. Ibid., (August 17, 1899), 3.

33. Ibid., (August 18, 1899), and SJN, III/103 (August 23, 1899), 4.

34. The New York Times, XLVIII (August 20, 1899), 7.

35. Ibid.

36. Ibid., (August 24, 1899), 12.

37. Knowlton Mixer. Porto Rico: history and conditions social, economic, and political. New York: MacMillan, 1926, p. 65.

38. SJN, IV/39 (January 25, 1900), 1. In 1901 the Woman's Aid Society sponsored Puerto Rican artists who gave a benefit performance. Arteaga was announced in El País, VII/95 (April 19, 1901), 3.

39. The New York Times, XLVIII (August 17, 1899), 3.

40. Ibid., (August 15, 1899), 4.

41. Ibid., XLIX (October 19, 1899), 1.

42. Ibid.

43. SJN, VIII/10 (January 14, 1903), supplement p. 1.

44. Ibid., VIII/83 (April 12, 1903), 3.

45. Ibid., VIII/215 (September 20, 1903), 3.

46. The Puerto Rico Herald, III/105 (August 1, 1903), 819-820, and III/106 (August 8, 1903), 835-6.

47. BM, LXVIII/259 (November 2, 1906), 5; LXVIII/267 (November 12, 1906), 5.

48. Ibid., LXVIII/276 (November 22, 1906), 5, and LXVIII/284 (December 1, 1906), 5.

49. United States Senate Document No. 5070, 59th Congress, 2nd Session, Document No. 135, p. 3.

50. Ibid., p. 4.

51. Ibid., Document No. 5070, Governor's Report, p. 11.

52. Ibid., p. 29.

53. BM, LXVIII/298 (December 18, 1906), 5.

PRESIDENT THEODORE ROOSEVELT TOURING THE ISLAND
(GEORGE CABOT WARD, second from the left)

CHAPTER IV

GEORGE CABOT WARD AND PUERTO RICAN SOCIETY

During this period when Puerto Rico passed from the Spanish to American control, there was inevitable friction between the functionaries and the people of the island. This was understandable, particularly because of the language barrier. The story of one appointed official and how he conquered Puerto Rican hostility is a refreshing episode in the island's history, and it indicates that some American officials were very much involved in the island's musical world. Throughout his term of office in the government, George Cabot Ward (1876-1936) and his wife, Justine Bayard Cutting Ward (1879-1975), showed an appreciation of the Puerto Rican culture and took a continuing interest in island activities. In 1905, when Ward was appointed Auditor of Puerto Rico by President Theodore Roosevelt, he and his wife moved to Old San Juan and occupied a house facing the Fortaleza. Ward arrived in Puerto Rico in February of 1906 and served as Auditor until August 30, 1909, when he was named Secretary of Puerto Rico by President William Howard Taft. Ward was Acting Governor at various times during his tenure as Secretary, the position he held until his resignation February 25, 1910.[1]

When the former Auditor, Thomas W. Hynes returned to the United States in November of 1905, he found illness in his family and resigned his position.[2] The following day, George Cabot Ward was named to succeed Hynes. When the news of Ward's appointment reached the island, The Puerto Rico Eagle stated that the new Auditor "is a young man of a very wealthy family of New York City and is a lawyer by profession."[3] Ward, who possessed a solid academic background, having graduated from Harvard College in 1898 and Harvard Law School in 1901, was admitted to the New York Bar in 1901, and practiced law in New York City before being appointed to his position in Puerto Rico.

He had been in Puerto Rico only five days when an editorial indicated that he had already favorably impressed the citizens. The affectionate "Salute" stated that Ward was an "exception to the general rule of bureaucrats"[4]--in the daily sessions of the

Executive Council, Ward was always present (according to the newspapers) and usually took an active role in the proceedings.

By March 31, Ward had proven himself worthy of even more favorable comments. The editorial bears repetition:

> "Let Mr. Post [Secretary and Acting Governor] profit by the lesson administered by the worthy councilor and learn to respect public opinion, to heed its dictates and obey its mandates; let him awaken to the necessity of satisfying an opinion that has the power and authority to impose its will.
>
> And it is not only Mr. Post--whose haughtiness and presumptions are proverbial--who should find in the Auditor an example worthy of emulation, there are others who hold the absurd view that everything foreign is superior to what is found here, that we must accept as great and unmerited favors all the capricious reforms and innovations imposed on us by the instruments of liquidation who masquerade as redeemers.
>
> How different our feeling and that of the general public would be toward the government, if among its members the same method of procedure adopted by Mr. Ward, the Auditor, was observed. Conscious of his unfamiliarity with questions relating to the colony, he refused to vote in the Executive Council a few hours after his arrival in the island, thus showing not only his good sense but also his respect for the country to which he had come."[5]

The Wards were immediately included in civic and church social functions. They attended a ceremony at the Collegio Sagrado Corazón at which the Bishop officiated, and during which the Police Band performed brilliant concert pieces.[6] During the next month, Mrs. Ward was named to the Board of Directors of the Anti-Tuberculosis League of Puerto Rico, along with the wife of Governor Beekman Winthrop and others.[7] On April 17, in the salón of Parque Borínquen, the Wards, along with the leaders of San Juan Society, attended a "Fancy Dress Ball." This must have been a very special occasion in their early San Juan days because Mrs. Ward's scrapbook of those years preserves many pictures of her "grandmother's dress," which she wore that evening.[8] The dance lasted from 9 p.m. until 2 a.m., with music by the orchestra of the Insular Police Band, Señor Francisco Verar conducting.[9]

Ward's first residence in Puerto Rico was on a side street facing the Governor's Palace. While they were in San Juan they occupied several houses, including the famous "Pink Palace" which was the home of the Secretaries of Puerto Rico. Their second home was on the sea wall near the Fortaleza. They also owned a home in the country where they could escape for fresh air and rest. Their cabin had originally been a road mender's cabin on the side of the mountain.

Apparently, when other United States-appointed officials arrived in San Juan they lived in government-owned homes. Several editorials appeared in the newspapers that spring criticizing the Secretary for living in the "Pink Palace" and other government officials who would not pay their utilities. The editorial stated that these people lived at the expense of the government and never purchased property on the island.[10] The first resident of the "Pink Palace" had been the Attorney General James Harlin, after whom, in October of 1901, it was occupied by Secretary Charles Hartzell and then by succeeding Secretaries.[11]

On May 21, 1906, Governor Beekman Winthrop returned to Puerto Rico and the "disturbing and alarming" term of Post was about to end.[12] The following day, however, when the Governor returned, he received a "glacial" reception from the people because so many unpleasant and disagreeable occurrences had taken place during his absence.[13] Post left for the States the next week (for a short stay) and the editor reported that he had left the country in a "near state of revolt."[14] With Post gone, Winthrop became the target of severe criticism by the news media. Clearly, leaders of the Puerto Rican society had lost confidence in him, although much of the problem was caused by Post.

"Then came Mr. Ward," declared the editor of the

Boletín Mercantil de Puerto Rico. From "the moment of his arrival," he demonstrated he was "a competent official and a distinguished administrator . . . . He respected the Puerto Rican people, and was the opposite of the typical imperialists who insisted on their ability to "instruct and enlighten" the natives "on all matters."[15]

At the end of June, Elihu Root, United States Scretary of State, stopped in San Juan for two days. On his way to Brazil on a diplomatic mission, Root came to Puerto Rico to study the situation on the island. A reception was given for him in the Palacio de Santa Catalina, summer residence for the occupants of the Fortaleza. The Insular Police Band played and the leaders of San Juan Society were invited.[16]

While in Puerto Rico, Root was quoted as declaring:

"I will do all that I can to have the American people concede to you the benefits which they enjoy and of which you are so deserving. . . ," one observer commented.

"It is very comforting and consoling to have a man of the standing and eminence of Mr. Root speak of the culture of our people and tell us, without repeating the old false legend of our lack of preparation that he will do his part toward having the American people grant us the same benefits which they enjoy.

After what has been said by the Secretary of State, it will not do for the bureaucrats of exportation to repeat their stupid and inharmonious refrain as justification for their intolerable usurpations."[17]

Soon after Root's departure, the editor again praised George Cabot Ward for his opposition to an economic proposal that was seen by natives as the epitome of imperialism. Yet, the editorial expressed concern that the other Americans on the Council were offended by Ward's approach.

"Quite likely, [they] have viewed with a fear amounting to horror what they doubtless judge to be the iconoclastic tendencies of the distinguished official who does not recognize in the reverend congregation the ineffable superiority which it believes itself to possess. [Yet,]

It is a matter of slight consequence what the congregantes think, their views and opinions carry no weight outside themselves; public opinion heartily endorses all that has been said by Mr. Ward and accords him enthusiastic praise.

In the public mind, the Auditor is separate and distinct from the congregation, he is a different type of man from the members of that mesocratic clique, he does not share the imperialistic and absorbing views of the bureaucracy; he seems to have a higher and more lofty ambition than those who have taken in charge the nefarious undertaking of effecting the liquidation of the island."[18]

In mid August, the Wards sailed for the United States, not only for a vacation but to enlighten the President on Puerto Rican problems.[19] He declared that the problems, both political and economic, could have been partially solved with recognition of Puerto Rico and complete citizenship for its people. Ward also reported the depression and poverty which existed in the coffee districts, due to "an unfair and unjust" tariff. Puerto Rico had been forced to consume only American products because of the tariff of that time. It seemed only just that an equal obligation should exist regarding the tariff which prevented Puerto Rican coffee from being imported into the United States.[20]

During the Wards' absence from Puerto Rico, it was announced that Governor Winthrop would be leaving, and there was speculation and hope that Ward might be his successor. He was praised for his "individual merit and ability," as a man "who, in no matter what position he may be placed, shows intelligence and fairness in all his acts."[21]

In November, when he returned to Puerto Rico, newspapers carried the story of his conference with Roosevelt, and about the $1,000,000 appropriated for

45

the construction of new roads.[22] Ward returned to
Puerto Rico amid preparations for Roosevelt's trip to
the island, and he was among the dignitaries to
accompany the president on his island tour.[23] The
next month Ward again demonstrated his genuine
concern for the local problems when he contributed to
a fiesta for the poor children of San Juan.[24] In
addition to his support by the public, as Auditor of
Puerto Rico, Ward demonstrated that he was
conscientious and efficient. He had made a close
study of the system of audit and found that it failed
to meet the requirements of the times. Indeed, by the
old system it was possible for the same bill to be
paid several times! Ward established a uniform system
for ordering goods, using duplicate forms. Apparently
improper payments had been made, payments in cash
instead of by check. He initiated a system of direct
audit before payment, he suggested an annual audit of
all books of all departments, and he revised the
bookkeeping system; thereafter a more complete record
of government business would exist.[25]

In 1907, Ward impressed the Puerto Rican people
with his determination to learn Spanish, which by
them he "spoke correctly and wrote with
elegance."[26] Moreover, he was concerned that
notices of public hearings were printed in English,
which meant that no local citizens would attend.[27]
Cognizant of this fact, Ward announced that his
reports would be printed in Spanish.[28] The editor
of the Boletín Mercantil de Puerto Rico again praised
Ward, noting the marked difference between his views
"and those who boast of their ignorance of the
language spoken in the colony and would abolish
it."[29]

As a member of the Executive Council, he proposed
bills to consider real estate decisions,[30] to
establish a special commission to study anemia among
the people,[31] and to provide compensation to
certain city councils of Puerto Rico for the
maintenance of city jails.[32] He recommended radical
changes in the system of auditing and accounting,
introducing more modern methods into the business
office of the Insular Government. He also created a
Paymaster's Bureau in the Treasury Department. He
suggested that the Fund of the Insular Police Band
which was used to purchase music, repair instruments,
and meet various band expenses be placed in the
Insular Treasury or be deposited with the Chief of

Police instead of remaining in the hands of the bandmaster. All in all, his office furnished more financial data than formerly, and the reports were published in the Official Gazette, a new government periodical.[33]

In March, when President Roosevelt cabled Governor Winthrop with the news that he was to become Under Secretary of the Treasury in Washington, it was speculated that Ward might be a possible candidate for Governor.[34] By March, however, Regis Post had been named Governor and Ward was now mentioned as a possible successor to Post as Secretary of Puerto Rico.[35] This was not to materialize for another two years.

Socially, in 1907 the Wards participated in many functions. On January 17 they attended a fiesta hosted by the Winthrops in the Executive Mansion, with entertainment by the Police Band.[36] On January 23 at the Hotel Inglaterra they attended a banquet in honor of the King of Spain, Don Alfonso XIII.[37] A sextet directed by Maestro Márquez played works by Sarasate, Leoncavallo, Wagner, Mascagni, Albeniz, Caballero, and Márquez; and several dignitaries gave speeches in Spanish including the Governor who recorded the glories of the discoveries of America. The next day the news media saluted all of the orators, especially the brilliant speech by Muñoz Rivera, and Ward, who pleased them all with his speech in correct Spanish.[38]

In February, the Wards participated in a carnival for the benefit of the Women's and Children's Hospital at which the Band of the Regiment of Puerto Rico and the Insular Police Band played. Mrs. Ward was listed among those at the "Kiosco de confeti," where they promoted a "battle of confetti."[39] There was also a vaudeville show with numbers sung by Amalia Paoli and piano solos by Monsita Ferrer.[40] The next week the Wards attended a dance in the Elks Club with the orchestra of the Police playing music by Juan Ríos Ovalle.[41]

In April they toured the island in an automobile caravan, escorting the Secretary of War, William Howard Taft and his wife,[42] and on their return attended a splendid banquet at the Executive Mansion in honor of the Tafts.[43]

The new Governor (Post) was inaugurated in the Municipal Theatre the next day and after a prayer by the Bishop, the Oath given by the President of the Supreme Court of Puerto Rico, a discourse by the Governor, and a review by the troops outside, the Secretary of War and ex-Governor Winthrop were escorted to their ship. An inaugural ball followed that evening.[44] On April 15 there was a reception in the gardens of the Fortaleza, before which there was a banquet at the Union Club.[45] The Tafts and the Winthrops were present as were members of the Executive Council and their wives and the leaders of San Juan Society. Finally, on April 18 the Tafts and the Winthrops left on the "Mayflower," with numerous officials and friends seeing them off. The Battalion of the Regiment of Puerto Rico formed on the Wharf and gave a parting salute to the dignitaries.[46]

In June of 1907, George Cabot Ward demonstrated that Puerto Rico was becoming modernized, when he issued an invitation to the people to join an Automobile Club. He was named president, and other officers were Luis Toro as Vice President, Edwin L. Arnold as Treasurer, and Charles Hartzell as Secretary.[47] They took auto trips to a fiesta in Ponce,[48] and in August they toured the island with the governor in the lead car. They reached Caguas in two hours and sixteen minutes, and in Aibonito in five hours and three minutes. Some of the cars broke down on the trip, and Ward's auto trouble prevented him from arriving at Coamo with the others.[49]

At the end of the summer the Wards left for the United States, returning to the island on December 5.[50] When Governor Post returned on the eleventh, Ward was among the dignitaries to meet him, and the Police Band played <u>La Borinqueña</u>.[51] Ward attended the banquet for Governor Post at which the Police Band played, and all important government employees were present.[52]

Rather significantly, when new Directors were named for the Ateneo Puertorriqueño, George Cabot Ward was elected to the Board, the only member who was not a native Puerto Rican. The new officers were President Ferdinand R. Cesteros, Vice President Emilio de Toro, and Board Members, George Cabot Ward, Federico Degetau, Jacinto Texidor, Manuel Vélez López, Rafael Monagas, V. Urrutia. The Secretary was José de Janer, Vice Secretary was Enrique Contreras,

Treasurer Manuel F. Calderón, and Librarian Rafael
Asenjo.[53] It was unprecedented for an American to
be accepted in such a way, and Ward attended all the
director's meetings and the social functions of the
organization.

The Wards were present at all important social
functions. When Julio Arteaga gave a recital of his
pupils in the salón of the Paris Bazaar, they heard
Mrs. Arteaga sing songs by her husband, Madrigal, and
Tu qui audio, and an aria by Rossini.[54] Ward was
always certain to write to express his appreciation
for being invited and he always complimented the
hosts and hostesses. For example, when Francisco
Verar conducted the Police Band at a reception the
Wards gave in their home, Ward sent a letter to Verar
thanking the band for the fine presentation, and for
the brilliant execution of the many compositions,
among which were danzas by "the immortal" Morel
Campos and his "illustrious successor" Juan Ríos
Ovalle. Ward's letter was printed in the
newspaper.[55] When the reporters mentioned Mrs.
Ward, she was always "la distinguida señora de Ward,"
and was always described as beautifully or elegantly
dressed with lovely embroidered work or many
brilliant jewels, or both.[56]

When a meeting was held of all of the officers of
the various societies of the city, Mrs. Ward was
elected a Vice President, and the other committee
members included Nicolasa Torruella de Arteaga, María
Amelia Pasarell, María Luisa Díaz Canaja, Josefina
Noble, and Mínima del Valle.[57]

The Wards were invited to the wedding of the
daughter of Pedro Giusti in the San Juan Cathedral
and a reception at "Villa Francia" in Hato Rey.[58]
When Julio Arteaga featured his daughter in a
recital, he invited the Wards to attend. Genoveva De
Arteaga performed a sonata by Reinecke. Srta. Belén
Dueño performed the Mozart Piano Concerto in A Major
and an Impromptu by Schubert. Mrs. Arteaga sang arias
by Mozart, Rossini, and Verdi.[59]

Ward was on hand for the celebration of the
Fourth of July and he joined the Governor in the
reviewing stand as the Regiment of Puerto Rico filed
by.[60] Later that month he and Mrs. Ward were in
Ponce for the weekend to attend the horse races.[61]
Returning to the city that attended a banquet in

honor of Governor Post, with the Police Orchestra in a side room playing musical selections.[62]

In August Mr. Ward participated in the Teacher Institute, as he had done in 1907. He briefly insisted on the need for cooperation of the parents--to assist the teachers in their work and help and encourage their children in their studies.[63]

At the meeting of the Ateneo Board of Directors, Ward gave a prize to the Puerto Rican composer of the winning danza in their contests.[64] He was reelected to the Board in 1908. The officers for the year were Ferdinand R. Cesteros as President, Vice President Emilio del Toro Cuebas, Treasurer Aureliano Ferrer Viale, Vice Treasurer Manuel R. Calderón, Secretaries Enrique Contreras and Arturo Córdova Landrón, Librarians Rafael E. Ramírez and A. López Tizol, Board Members, Martín Travieso, Jr., Rafael Monagas, Eugenio G. de Hostos, George Cabot Ward, Augusto Malaret, and José Janer. Again, a great honor was extended to Ward, the only American on the Board.[65]

In his final report as Auditor in 1908, Ward boasted many improvements in methods in Government Bureaus. It was during this time that the Legislature appropriated the $200,000 settlement for the Catholic Church against the Insular Government. The first $60,000 was paid in 1908-9 and the remainder during the next two years, with interest. Official automobiles were now being provided, enabling officials to reach more places efficiently. Ward created a new bureau of traveling examiners, a unified system of accounting, and he continued to work on the reorganization of the Auditor's office.[66]

At the end of August he was named Secretary of Puerto Rico by President Taft.[67] Ward received numerous letters, cablegrams, and communications of congratulations from his friends in the United States and around the island. By October he was Acting Governor. In this capacity he had to prepare the program of activities for the newly-named Governor, George Colton, who was to arrive from the United States on November 4.[68] While Ward was Acting Governor, his father-in-law, William Bayard Cutting, gave $500 to the Anti-Tuberculous League of Puerto Rico. In the same article in which that gift was announced, the Acting Governor informed the reporter that he had given a silver cup to the President of the Ateneo Puertorriqueño to be awarded to the composer of a Puerto Rican danza, as a prize for excellence in the contests of the Ateneo.[69]

The Wards greeted the new Governor and his family as they disembarked from the "Morro Castle,"[70] and gave a reception for them in the "palacio rojo," the "Pink Palace," home of the Secretary of Puerto Rico.[71] After the inauguration a letter was published in the newspaper signed by George Cabot Ward in which he expressed his profound gratitude to all who contributed to the success of the ceremonies. It was a warm, gracious, thoughtful letter. No other Governor had ever written such a communication to the people.[72]

Ward left for the United States for a minor operation in December. In his absence, Mrs. Ward assisted with a program to benefit poor children. She was also on the Board of Directors for the Society to assist the poor.[73] When he returned, he and Mrs. Ward attended a fiesta in the Hippodrome for the benefit of the hearing impaired.[74]

Both George Ward and his wife were musicians. By profession he was a lawyer, but he also played the violin. In fact, early in his career he had been advised by the celebrated lawyer and ambassador to England Joseph Choate, "Never let anyone know that you play the violin; it would wreck your career!"[75]

Justine Bayard Cutting Ward, who later in life created what became known as The Ward Method of School Music,[76] was the daughter of William Bayard Cutting, a boxholder in the Old Academy of Music and a member of the Board of Directors of the Metropolitan Opera Company of New York. She was an accomplished pianist, had been schooled privately by tutors, and had attended the Brearly School in New York. She had been a personal friend of Father William O'Brien Pardow, S.J., whose biography she later wrote, and who converted her to Catholicism on June 27, 1904 at Saint Ignatius Loyola Church on Park Avenue in New York.[77]

Justine Ward had become interested in the plainsong of the Church and had studied the rhythm of the chant with Father J.B. Young of Saint Francis

Xavier Church in New York City. Father Young had developed a system of sight reading and singing, a new plan of studies for the parochial schools of the Archdiocese of New York. Justine Ward later adopted his tonal exercises.

After the Papal encyclical of Pius X, the _Motu Proprio_ of November 22, 1903, Justine Ward began writing about Church music. By the time she arrived in Puerto Rico she was already recognized as a rising author. Her article, "Church or Concert," originally published in _The Messenger_ (1905), was translated into German and printed in the _Augsburger Postzeitung_ (1906). Her article, "The Reform in Church Music," which first appeared in the _Atlantic Monthly_ (April, 1906), was reprinted as a booklet by London's Catholic Truth Society, and was also printed by _The Messenger_ (No. 12, June 22, 1906), and in Philadelphia by _Education Briefs_ (No. 24, October, 1908).

Concerning this last article, "The Reform in Church Music," she received several letters of commendation which she preserved in her scrapbooks. A letter from Professor John Singenberger (Sacred Heart Sanitarium, Wisconsin, June 21, 1906) inquired if he might have permission to reprint the article for his readers. Mrs. Ward also received a request from Father Joseph Nieborowski of Térraba (Costa Rica) to publish the work in Spanish. The editor of _The Messenger_ wrote to her stating that readers had written suggesting that the article be reproduced and widely disseminated.[78] Edith Wharton wrote a note to her praising her endeavors,[79] and a friend from Pallous had the article bound in white and gold with a fine silk book mark and sent it to the Pope, who responded that he would read it that evening (July 25, 1908).[80]

Federico Degetau, the First Commissioner from Puerto Rico to the United States Congress, wrote a letter to Mrs. Ward acknowledging the receipt of this article, which he planned to translate into Spanish.[81] His translation, "La reforma de la Música Religiosa," was published in _La Verdad, Revista Católica de San Juan, P.R._ (June 27, 1908). Degetau read his translation at the meeting of the Ateneo Puertorriqueño honoring the memory of Felipe Gutiérrez.[82] During the evening the Insular Police Orchestra, directed by Francisco Verar, played the

Overture from Guarionex by Gutiérrez, followed by a speech by the Vice President of the Ateneo, Emilio de Toro Cuebas. The orchestra then played El Parto de los montes, a capricho with clarinet and flute obligato by Gutiérrez. Manuel Fernández Juncos gave a reading followed by the study on Gregorian Chant by Justine B. Ward, read by Degetau.

After the intermission, the orchestra played La Familia, a symphony by Gutiérrez. Rafael Monagas described the life of Gutiérrez, Mrs. Arteaga sang Elegy by Massenet and Quanti Mai by Gounod, and Julio Arteaga played the Appasionata Sonata, Op. 57, by Beethoven. José Janer gave a poetry reading and the evening ended with the orchestra playing the grand march from Meyerbeer's El Profeta.[83]

Copies of the study by Mrs. Ward were given to the audience, and she received great applause. Later Manuel Fernández Juncos reviewed Mrs. Ward's study in Cervantes and he wrote that it was a "very spiritual paper, aesthetically profound," and praised Mrs. Ward for her "great sincerity, her intellectual ability, her sharp ingenuity which enabled her to express herself so elegantly."[84]

When Ward resigned as Secretary of Puerto Rico on February 25, 1910,[85] he told a reporter that he would leave Puerto Rico "with profound sadness. I have spent four years here . . . . everyday I appreciate more the hospitality of the Puerto Rican people."[86]

When the Wards left Puerto Rico, a newspaper mentioned that the Wards would be missed in the highest social circles.[87] Governor Colton gave a luncheon for Ward on March 9, 1910. The Colonial Regiment of Puerto Rico, the Commander of the Marines, the President of the Supreme Court, and the members of the Executive Council and city leaders were all invited. They wished him success in his future political career, and he declared that he would never forget his four years in Puerto Rico and the hospitality of the people. He praised the Council and the Administration of Governor Colton.[88]

Justine Ward went on to teach at Manhattanville College of the Sacred Heart and to found the Pius X School of Liturgical Music at that college. Because of their friendship with the Wards when they were in

Puerto Rico, both Julio Arteaga and his daughter Genoveva attended the Pius X School of Liturgical Music in 1921.[89]

The Wards were missed in Puerto Rico. About June of 1910 a letter to La Correspondencia de Puerto Rico inquired whether there were still a Club Automovilista since Cabot Ward had left. Since he had founded it and was its president, the reader wondered what had happened to the organization. The reporter informed him that the club was still functioning and that the dues for active members were $25 to join and $40 for the year.[90]

That year, Ward was a member of the United States Delegation to the Fourth Pan American Congress at Buenos Aires, in July, and a member of the United States Commission to Chile. He served as Commissioner of Parks of New York City from 1914 to 1917.[91] As Park Commissioner he urged the organization of a permanent committee of citizens to combat any attempt to invade the parks and he opened a campaign to remove large advertising signs from city playgrounds. Resigning in November,[92] he was commissioned a Captain of the Ninth Coast Artillery, New York, and a Major in the Aviation Section Signal Corps. He was appointed assistant chief of staff and chief of the Intelligence Section, Line of Communication, A.E.F., on December 24, 1917. He was made a lieutenant colonial March 1, 1918.

Colonel Ward was a director of the American Library of Paris, of the Franco-American Society, of the Franco-American Welfare, and of France Amérique. He was a vice president of the Interallied Veterans Federation, chairman of the American Legion delegation to Brussels in 1922, a commander of the Serbian Order of the White Eagle, a member of the Political Science Association, the Bar Association of the City of New York, the American Association for Labor Legislation, the Pan-American Society and the Ibero-American Society.

Colonel Ward belonged to the University, Century, City, Republican, Bankers, Harvard, and Whitehall Clubs of New York, and to the Cosmos and Chevy Chase Clubs in Washington, D.C. Until his death in 1936, he made his home at 21 Avenue de la Victoire, Nice, France.[93]

NOTES

1. Before his tenure as Auditor, George Ward may have previously visited the island. On April 12, 1901, a J.G. Ward arrived on the "Philadelphia." (Often in the Puerto Rican newspapers his name was printed as Jorge or Jacob.) According to SJN, VI/86 (April 13, 1901), 8, in March, 1904, a Mr. Ward left for the North on the "Ponce," according to SJN, IX/62 (March 16, 1904), 3.

2. BM, LXVII/275 (November 29, 1905), 7, and LXVII/276 (November 30, 1905), 6, and LaC, XVI (December 28, 1905), 6.

3. The Puerto Rico Eagle, IV (December 30, 1905), 8. The report speculated that the new Auditor would arrive early in the month. The BM, LXVIII/5 (January 6, 1906), 4, stated that Ward would leave for Puerto Rico, sailing on the 27th, and BM, LXVIII/24 (January 29, 1906), 4, stated that he had left New York for the Island. Ibid., LXVIII/27 (February 1, 1906), 7, stated that he would leave New York the next day. The Puerto Rico Eagle, IV (February 12, 1906), 8, stated that he would leave on the next ship, and the same paper, IV (February 24, 1906), 8, stated that he had arrived on the "Coamo." BM, LXVIII/45 (February 23, 1906), 7, listed the Honorable George Cabot Ward and maid among the passengers of the "Philadelphia" and page 4 carried the story of his arrival on that ship. Other articles about his appointment appeared in the BM, LVII/298 (December 28, 1905), 7, and LaC, XVI (December 29, 1905), 2.

4. BM, LXVIII/49 (February 28, 1906), 2.

5. Ibid., LXVIII/76 (March 31, 1906), 5.

6. Ibid., LXVIII/67 (March 21, 1906), 2, and LXVIII/60 (March 13, 1906), 1. There were musical numbers, poetry, a discourse by the Bishop and a final hymn accompanied by the orchestra.

7. Ibid., LXVIII/78 (April 3, 1906), 1.

8. Scrapbooks are not named nor are the pages numbered.

9. BM, LXVIII/89 (April 17, 1906), 6. Special mention of Mrs. Ward's dress was noted here.

10. Ibid., LXVIII/106 (May 7, 1906), 5.

11. Ibid., LXVIII/104 (May 5, 1906), 5.

12. Ibid., LXVIII/119 (May 21, 1906), 5.

13. Ibid., LXVIII/123 (May 25, 1906), 5.

14. Ibid., LXVIII/127 (May 31, 1906), 5.

15. Ibid., LXVIII/111 (May 14, 1906), 5.

16. Ibid., LXVIII/152 (June 29, 1906), 5; LXVIII/165 (July 10, 1906), 2. and LXVIII/161 (July 11, 1906), 2.

17. Ibid., LXVIII/163 (July 13, 1906), 2.

18. Ibid., LXVIII/167 (July 18, 1906), 2.

19. Ibid., LXVIII/190 (August 14, 1906), 4.

20. Ibid., LXVIII/210 (September 6, 1906), 5. Several articles sang his praises, including LXVIII/209 (September 5, 1906), 2, and LXVIII/210 (September 6, 1906), 2.

21. Ibid., LXVIII/234 (October 4, 1906), 6, also LXVIII/233 (October 3, 1906), 2.

22. Ibid., LXVIII/260 (November 3, 1906), 5.

23. Ibid., LXVIII/277 (November 23, 1906), 7. Pictures from Justine Ward's scrapbook.

24. Ibid., LXVIII/307 (December 29, 1906), 2.

25. United States House of Representatives Document Vol. 49, No. 5152--59th Congress, 2nd Session. Document No. 203, p. 73. Annual Report of the Auditor of Puerto Rico to the Governor for the Fiscal Year Ending June 30, 1906.

26. BM, LXXII/56 (March 8, 1910), 2.

27. Ibid., LXVIII/114 (May 16, 1906), 5. This was an editorial relating to the Commissioner of the Interior and the fact that an interpreter was employed at all proceedings of the Council, but the announcements were always in English.

28. LaC, XVII (January 7, 1907), 3.

29. RM, LXIX/7 (January 9, 1907), 5.

30. Ibid., LXIX/24 (January 29, 1907), 4.

31. LaC, XVII (February 4, 1907), 3.

32. Ibid., (March 1, 1907), 2, and (March 5, 1907), 2.

33. Second Annual Report of the Auditor of Puerto Rico for the Fiscal Year Ending June 30, 1907. House Document Vol. 49, No. 5152--59th Congress, 2nd Session. Document No. 203, pp. 1-33.

34. BM, LXIX/54 (March 5, 1907), 2, 5.

35. LaC, XVII (March 8, 1907), 1.

36. Ibid., (January 18, 1907), 2.

37. Ibid., (January 24, 1907), 2.

38. BM, LXIX/20 (January 24, 1907), 2.

39. LaC, XVII (February 6, 1907), 2.

40. Ibid., (February 7, 1907), 2.

41. Ibid., (February 12, 1907), 2.

42. BM, LXIX/89 (April 10, 1907), 2.

43. Ibid., LXIX/80 (April 12. 1907), 2, and LaC, XVII (April 12, 1907), 3.

44. BM, LXIX/87 (April 13, 1907), 2.

45. LaC, XVII (April 16, 1907), 1, 2.

46. BM, LXIX/91 (April 18, 1907), 2.

47. LaC, XVII (January 25, 1907), 3.

48. Ibid., (July 25, 1907), 3.

49. Ibid., (August 16, 1907), 21 (August 17 (1907), 2, and (August 19, 1907), 2.

50. Ibid., (November 26, 1907), 2, and (December 6, 1907), 3.

51. Ibid., (December 12, 1907), 1.

52. Ibid., (December 16, 1907), 1.

53. Ibid., (December 30, 1907), 3.

54. Ibid., (January 24, 1908), 4.

55. Ibid., (February 28, 1908), 2.

56. Ibid., (February 26, 1908), 3, and (February 7, 1908), 2.

57. Ibid., (May 9, 1908), 3.

58. Ibid., (May 12, 1908), 2.

59. Ibid., (June 4, 1908), 1.

60. BM, LXX/158 (July 6, 1908), 2.

61. Ibid., LXX/173 (July 24, 1908), 2.

62. Ibid., LXX/178 (July 29, 1908), 2.

63. United States Senate Document No. 5393--60th Congress, 2nd Session, Annual Report of the Governor. Document No. 578, pp. 208-9. In 1907, Ward, Rafael del Valle, and Manuel Fernández Juncos addressed the group. Also see BM, LXX/184 (August 5, 1908), 2.

64. Ibid., p. 3, and LXX/282 (December 24, 1908), 2.

65. Ibid., LXX/285 (December 29, 1908), 3. According to the Junta Directiva y Presidentes de Secciones of the Ateneo for 1909, he was elected on December 28, 1908.

66. Annual Report of the Auditor of Puerto Rico for the Fiscal Year Ending June 30, 1909, United States Senate Document No. 5393--60th Congress, 2nd Session. Document No. 578, pp. 4-25.

67. BM, LXXI/207 (August 25, 1909), 2.

68. LaC, XIX (October 15, 1909), 2, and (October 20, 1909), 2.

69. Ibid., (October 23, 1909), 6.

70. LaC, XIX (November 5, 1909), 2.

71. Ibid., (November 9, 1909), 2.

72. Ibid., (November 18, 1909), 2.

73. Ibid., (December 2, 1909), 6, and (December 7, 1909), 7, and Ibid., which stated that he would return on the 18th (December 15, 1909), 2.

74. Ibid., (December 20, 1909), 5.

75. Iris Orrigo. _Images and Shadows_. New York: Harcourt Brace Javanovich, Inc., 1970, p. 30.

76. _The Ward Method/Music Instruction for Catholic Schools. Grades 1-8_. Washington, D.C.: The Catholic University of America Press for the Center for Ward Studies, 1976.

77. New York: Longmans, Green & Co., 1915.

78. John S. Wynne, S.J., Kohlman Hall, Fort Washington Avenue at 181st Street, April 27, 1906.

79. Orrigo, p. 30. She wrote that one day when Justine was a young girl her mother invited Edith Wharton to see a tapestry which was in the drawing room where Justine was Practicing the piano. Mrs. Wharton's remark was, "Well, Teddy, it may be just as well that we never had any children. Just think, one of them might have been musical!"

80. Letter unsigned, but the information under the picture of Pallous castle shows that her "Aunt" Schoenberg lived there.

81. Letter in her scrapbook.

82. _LaC_, XVIII (June 13, 1908), 1.

83. _Ibid._, (June 15, 1908), 2.

84. "Una precioso estudio sobre música religiosa," _Cervantes, Revista Decenal de Literature, Ciencias y Artés_, IV/23 (July 10, 1908), 1-4.

85. _BM_, LXXII/47 (February 25, 1910), 2.

86. _Ibid._, LXXII/48 (February 26, 1910), 2.

87. _Ibid._, LXXII/56 (March 8, 1910), 2.

88. _Ibid._, LXXII/57 (March 9, 1910), 2.

89. Personal letter, May 23, 1976.

90. _LaC_, XX (June 20, 1910), 1.

91. _The New York Times_, (August 28, 1915), 14.

92. _Ibid._, (November 14, 1917), 15.

93. _Ibid._, (May 14, 1936), 25.

CHAPTER V

THE PUBLIC SCHOOLS AND MUSIC IN THE CURRICULUM

When Puerto Rico was colonized by the Spaniards, missionaries of the Roman Catholic Church accompanied them, and schools of a religious nature were established.[1] They were not intended to benefit the poor, however; they were for the wealthy planters who could contribute to the church. No specific sum for education was found in the records of 1842, when the sum of $300 was set aside to pay for schooling of ten girls each year.[2] The old colonial records do not state how long this practice was continued, but they do show that a rudimentary school system had existed as early as 1820. The teachers were nuns and the curriculum was determined by the church. During that period no one is known to have devoted his life to teaching. Expenditures were met as the need demanded.

On October 30, 1898, twelve days after the arrival of the United States Military Government, at a mass meeting in San Juan, a series of resolutions were adopted, including one which related to public education[3] The resolution asserted that the best way to improve conditions was to establish kindergartens for the very young and normal schools to train the teachers, just as existed in the United States. The elementary schools were to be graded and to utilize modern methods and materials. Schools for adults, Sunday schools, art and trade schools, libraries, museums, academies of fine arts, and literary clubs were also to be established. Education was to be compulsory and free. Grades of instruction were to be on three levels; fundamental or elementary, secondary for instruction in scientific, civic, and technical subjects; professional, including law, medicine, engineering, and technology; and university, for advanced work in science. In order to assure the competency of teachers, normal schools would be established to train teachers and professors. Military and naval schools were also to be established. Since the resolutions were adopted so soon after the military takeover, it appears certain that an interest in education existed in Puerto Rico before the American occupation.

With the American takeover, there were no more government scholarships to enable young musicians to study in Europe. Nevertheless, it could be said that children had the most to gain from the new government. According to historian María M. Brau, "Even at its worst, American military rule was far better than Spanish rule. There was freedom of the press, freedom of association, and freedom of worship . . . . Free public schooling was made compulsory, and free textbooks were provided. Schools were built . . . ."[4]

According to the Annual Report of the Governor of Puerto Rico, showing "The Progress of a Decade, 1899-1908,"[5] at the same time of American occupation there were 380 "public schools" for boys, 148 for girls, and one for adults. There were also 26 private schools, for a total of 555 "schools." The "public schools" enrolled a total of 25,664 children. Although there were "public schools," there were no buildings; classes were held in the teachers' homes.[6] In 1899 there was only one school in all of Puerto Rico, but 1912 there were 1168 public schools, most in buildings of their own. The United States Government spent $11,691,349 in order to educate the children.[7]

Where the district provided only one school, the school was open to both sexes. The school year was limited to nine months of twenty days each. The number of pupils for each teacher was limited to fifty. The course of study included the required subjects--Spanish, English, arithmetic, geography, United States history, and civil government. The minor subjects were music, hygiene, morals, and manual training. Church doctrine and religion disappeared from the curriculum.[8]

An article that appeared in The New York Times stated that the Puerto Rican people had made clear that they favored the establishment of free public non sectarian schools, sufficient to give every child the opportunity for a good education. They believed that the English language should be taught in all of the schools in order to prepare these children for a better place in society.[9] The school hours were long enough to enable pupils to prepare lessons at school. The program of daily work was to be posted in each classroom and strictly followed.

By January 5, 1900, the total enrollment in the schools was 31,000 pupils, at a cost of $13.38 per pupil. There still remained, however, 268,680 children without the opportunity to attend school. Textbooks were in English and Spanish. Where there were no textbooks, in the girls' schools, the students learned embroidery.[10] In January a new model school and training school was opened. The flag was raised and the children sang the Star Spangled Banner and Columbia the Gem of the Ocean. According to the newspaper, this was the first building erected by the Americans in Puerto Rico in which to teach children by American methods. There were twelve grades in the school, and 350 children in attendance.[11]

In 1900, Puerto Rican teachers were sent to study at Harvard at the expense of the government.[12] Many colleges in the United States offered reduced tuition to Puerto Rican students and the following colleges and universities admitted them free of tuition: Amherst, Cornell, Georgetown, Haverford, Hobart, Hampden-Sidney, Lehigh, the New York State Normal School at Genesee, Syracuse, Virginia Polytechnic Institute, Williams, and Yale.[13] That fall a normal school opened in Fajardo with Dr. E.E. Riopel as Principal. Subjects taught were Spanish, English, pedagogy, history of education, mathematics, physics, history, physical and descriptive geography, biology, geology, music, drawing, clay work, and reed or basket weaving.[14]

According to María Luisa Muñoz, in the period following 1898 there were many school bands,[15] and Robert Fitzmaurice claims that there is evidence of instrumental music being taught in the schools. At the time of his dissertation there was a picture in the University of Puerto Rico [Río Piedras] Library, dated November 3, 1900, showing a band of thirteen boys and their director. According to Fitzmaurice, this was the Boys' Charity School Band in Santurce, in military style uniform.[16] According to Callejo, school bands were organized in towns and were supported by the school boards,[17] and the first school band festival recorded was held in 1910 in San Juan, with the bandas escolares participating.[18]

With music classes and singing in the schools, music became an indispensable part of holiday celebrations. These events generated closer ties between the schools and the public.[19] Music was included in the course of study in both the primary and intermediate grades since the beginning of the organization of schools. In 1899 a suggested outline for a course of study for grades I through VI was given to the teachers. Music as well as English had a prominent place in the curriculum.[20]

The first school programs that showed the adoption of the new holidays were for Washington's birthday. Preparations were made in early February, and the program was to be in English and Spanish. An announcement appeared in the newspaper stating that Army officers would prepare the program and that children would be taught a number of patriotic songs.[21] The Society of Sons of the Revolution of the State of New York provided pamphlets of three songs in Spanish and English--America, Columbia the Gem of the Ocean, and the Star Spangled Banner--in honor of the 168th anniversary of the birth of George Washington. These were used at the ceremonies.[22] During one of the programs at which General George W. Davis and Bishop Jaime Huberto Blenk made speeches, the children sang the three songs.[23] In the evening there was entertainment and dancing in the theatre, with music by the Eleventh Infantry Band.[24]

At the celebration in the American Missionary Association School in Santurce a Venezuelan song was sung in Spanish and several songs were sung in English, including Mount Vernon's Bells, The Red, White, and Blue, Flag of the Free, and the Battle Hymn of the Republic.[25] On the closing day of the school year, at Miss Anna Gould's Kindergarten, Cecilia Bruno sang La Borinqueña.[26]

During the 1900-1901 school year, Washington's birthday was widely celebrated with songs, poems, and band music. By the end of the school year it was reported that the children in the Caguas District were singing two-part music under the direction of Nina Piey,[27] and at Lares, the practicing of musical instruments could be heard all day long. There the children played everything from violins to bass horns.[28] Flag Day was celebrated that year with programs at the schools in Ponce, Caguas, Arecibo, Lares, Mayagüez, and Vega Baja.[29] The schools in Puerta de Tierra organized a fiesta in the theatre, and the program began with the Boys' Charity School Band playing a two-step, under the direction of the conductor, Juan Viñolo.[30]

Music was included in the school curriculum for the year 1901-1902. The Course of Study and Duties of Teachers for that year gives the following instructions:[31]

Primary Grades

First Year: Popular Songs, Breathing Exercises and Calisthenics

Second Year: Music Reading

Third Year: Popular Songs and Knowledge of Elements of Music

Fourth Year: Popular Songs and attention given to notation

Intermediate Grades

Fifth Grade: Music and Calisthenics

Sixth Grade: Music and Calisthenics

Seventh Grade: Music and Calisthenics

Eighth Grade: Exercises in Music and Calisthenics

At the end of the school year, Flag Day was again observed with a parade of school children from Plaza Colón to the Plaza Principal, followed by a program in the theatre. The Boys' Charity School Band played and there were recitations about the flag, drills, and patriotic songs sung by the children of Lincoln, McKinley, William Penn, Colón, and Ponce de León Schools.[32] The celebrations in July opened with a ball on the evening of the Fourth. The next day there was a parade at 9 a.m. with military and civil groups participating, followed by an afternoon program in the theatre, during which there were prayers, English and Spanish speeches, and a reading of the Declaration of Independence, and instrumental and vocal music. In the afternoon there was a baseball game followed by aquatic sports at the marina--a boat race for the girls and a double scull race for the boys. There was a greased pole in front of the Customs House, a 100 yard dash for the men, a sack race, a three legged race, and a blind chicken contest. Fireworks followed in the evening. The

65

Committee requested that all private residences be decorated with flags and bunting and that everybody take part in the celebration.[33]

During the next school year, Arbor Day was observed in the schools all over the island. There were songs, speeches, and recitations,[34] and special note was made of a new teacher of music, Miss Anderson of Santurce, who had graduated from the New York Grand Conservatory of Music and who had studied at the Royal Conservatory of Leipzig. She was teaching music in Santurce.[35]

The Report of the English Supervisor, E.E. Riopel of Ponce, predicted that English would become the language of the island, if the desire to learn it continued. He noted with surprise the people's devotion toward everything concerning their newly-adopted country. He stated that teachers and pupils alike were striving to learn English and that they took every opportunity, even at great disadvantage, to use it. He noted the general interest in securing an education among all of the people. His comments bear repetition here:

> "Parents plead for the admission of their children into the school when told there is no room. Mothers and fathers ford swollen rivers with their children on their backs to and from school, or they carry them miles over roads impassable for the child. Children go without their meals in order to obtain an education. Such devotion is not to be found in every quarter of the globe.
>
> Patriotism is displayed on every hand. Every schoolhouse has its floating stars and stripes. On the death of any prominent official of the government it is always flown at half-mast. They love to sing the songs of the nation and enter most heartily into that grand hymn, My Country 'tis of thee. The people love to cheer, "Viva America," "Viva los Estados Unidos," and I believe that they do this with even more heartfelt thanks than our own boys. As some of the older ones express themselves, they feel that the atmosphere is free, free from foreign oppression."[36]

Progress in educational matters was uninterrupted since the establishment of civil government in 1900. Dr. M.G. Brumbaugh was the first presidential appointee to the position of Commissioner of Education of Puerto Rico. He was one of the best known educators in the United States, having done graduate work at Harvard and the University of Pennsylvania, and possessing both a Ph.D. and L.L.D. He established a graded school system at the Charity School Building, starting from Kindergarten and continuing through the third year of high school.[37] He was succeeded in February, 1902, by Dr. Samuel McCune Lindsay, a well-known educator, sociologist, and author, and later Professor of Social Legislation at Columbia University (1908).[38] Lindsay oversaw the construction of more graded schools and the completion of the normal school, which in 1902 had been moved from Fajardo to Río Piedras.

The normal school was functioning well by March of 1903, when it presented a special program for Alice Roosevelt, who was visiting the island.[39] According to The San Juan News, when the new school year opened in September, the University of Puerto Rico was inaugurated but only the normal department opened that year.[40] The department had a glee club which rehearsed every Friday. At Thanksgiving a program consisting of songs and recitations was presented in the normal school. Everyone sang Our Country, followed by an address in Spanish.[41]

The various school festivals were celebrated in the different municipalities of the island with varying degrees from simple to quite elaborate. Exercises for George Washington's birthday in 1903 in the McKinley School were quite Americanized:[42]

Song: Washington
American Flag Salute (Spanish exercise) by six
          children
Composition: The Rose and Its Thorns by Mercedes
          Asenjo
Recitation: The American Flag by Aurora Álvarez
Composition: George Washington by Alberto G.
          Quevedo
Hymn: Washington
Composition: The Life of Washington by Manuel G.
          Quevedo
Recitation: The Nest by Carmen Castro
Dialogue: The Boy George Washington by 5 pupils

Composition: <u>George Washington</u> by Juanna Agiar
Address: <u>Senor Juan Hernández López</u>
Song: <u>Star Spangled Banner</u>

In Cayey during the same week, the musical program for George Washington given by the children in the public schools included the singing of <u>America</u>, and the school orchestra played the Puerto Rican national hymn, <u>La Borinqueña</u>.[43] For Flag Day that year, 1500 children from Colón, Lincoln, and McKinley Schools led by their teachers paraded in the street. The Insular Police Band played. "When the band struck up the music every little urchin began to wave his American flag keeping time to the music and jugging along in the procession."[44] That evening, in the Theatre when the Police Band ended its program it played "the dearly beloved <u>Borínquen</u>."[45]

During her trip to the island, Alice Roosevelt was the guest at many receptions, starting with one in the gardens of the summer palace in Río Piedras.[46] The governor's family escorted her to Ponce, with stops in Caguas and Cayey.[47] She had been invited to lay the corner-stone of the Roosevelt Industrial School in Ponce. All of the island officials, as well as teachers and children, came out to meet her. At the ceremonies the Bomberos Band played the opening greeting and the school children sang <u>America</u>.[48] A splendid buffet of various ices and champagne was provided, while the Insular Police Band entertained. The guests danced to an orchestra of five violins, one oboe, one flute, two clarinets, two trombones, two cornets, a contrabass, and one kettledrum. D. Eduardo Cuevas had composed a piece especially for the occasion, <u>Sinfonía Lazos de Amor</u>, and the orchestra played it.[49]

Alice left Ponce with Governor William Henry Hunt, Lieutenant Moreno, and Secretary Bliss, riding horseback from Cayey to Guayama. When they returned to Ponce, they were welcomed by a band in the Plaza.[50] On the drive to the home of the Mayor of Mayagüez, the Governor's party included 64 coaches followed by a guard of honor.[51] All over the island people had been well prepared for her visit. Her picture had been printed in many editions of the newspapers since her father was sworn in as President in 1901. The people were well aware of her by the time of her visit and they greeted her as an honored guest.

As far as programs in the elementary schools are concerned, in 1903 music was not mentioned in the Course of Study for the first two grades. Third and Fourth grade teachers, however, were advised to continue teaching songs as well as the fundamentals of music.[52] Programs continued in both English and Spanish, and Puerto Rican holidays were still observed, such as Columbus Day, November 19, in honor of the discovery of Puerto Rico.[53]

Arbor Day also called for a celebration in most schools. The Escuela Colón presented an impressive program in 1903.[54] The band directed by Manuel Tizol played an overture, followed by a selection, Les fleurs. Manuel Fernández Juncos delivered a speech and the program closed with the singing of La Borinqueña. At McKinley and several other schools in San Juan, poems were recited in English and Spanish, at Río Piedras there was music, songs, mandolin solos, and of course, the planting of trees.[55]

In 1903, a reporter praised the public schools as well as the teacher-training school which had been established in Río Piedras. He admitted that the United States was advancing the cause of education and sanitation, but noted that Spain had previously provided financial aid in various ways.[56]

Yet, it was obvious that efforts were being made to improve the quality of teaching. In the beginning, educators from the States were sent to assist native teachers, and during the summer of 1904 the United States Department of Education organized an eight-week trip [on Army transports] for Puerto Rican teachers for the purpose of study at Harvard and Cornell.[57] A total of 504 teachers took advantage of that opportunity, even though they had to contribute one month's salary (approximately $100) to help cover the cost, which included meals, lodging. tuition, and travel to Boston, Philadelphia, New York, and Washington. Over $20,000 was contributed by the people of Boston, New York, and Philadelphia, half coming from Boston as a result of the endorsement of President Charles Eliot of Harvard. It was reported that the Puerto Rican danza had taken hold on the Americans and that on one occasion they ended their evening amusement with one of their native waltzes; the Bostonians showed a curious delight in watching them dance.[58]

According to the Report of the Commissioner of Education, Roland F. Faulkner, in 1906 the instruction in the public schools was in Spanish and English taught as a special subject.[59] His report included the following chart of the number of schools on the island. Many of these "schools" apparently were contained in a single room.

Year		Number of Schools	
	Graded	Rural	Common
1901-2	381	490	871
1902-3	427	850	1007
1903-4	497	563	1063
1904-5	494	554	1048
1905-6	532	542	1074
Teachers in charge			
of the schools at the end of the fiscal year			
1906	503	497	1050
Schools at the end of the fiscal year			
1906	527	523	1050

Although there were schools, there was very little opportunity for most natives. At the commencement of the Normal School, Governor Beekman Winthrop told the graduates that there were only two fields open to them--Chemistry and School Teaching. Agriculture was not an option except to those who owned land.

The Editor of the Boletín Mercantil de Puerto Rico reported the Governor's speech and lamented the fact that the future would be grim for the coming generations. He was grateful that the Governor had spoken the truth but fearful that future graduates would not be ready to face what destiny had in store for them--"cruel awakenings and the most profound disillusionment."[60]

The Governor's 1907 Report to the United States Congress stated that only 84 Puerto Rican teachers were graduates of the colleges or normal schools and that 35 others had had some college or normal school training in addition to their other qualifications.[61] Teachers also went to Puerto Rico

70

from all sections of the Union. That year there were 119 teachers from 26 states and the District of Columbia.

According to his report, English was becoming a prominent language and this had made selection of teachers an essential factor for the success of the program. However, all teachers were expected to acquire a knowledge of Spanish in order to communicate with their students.

Although there was a large number of elementary schools, and an increasing number of teachers, in 1907 there were high schools in only three cities on the island.[62] In that year, the legislature appropriated funds for fifty scholarships, to be distributed among the towns to allow students to attend these schools. The legislature also appropriated $80,000 for the construction of school buildings. By 1908, scholarships in the high schools were increased to $100 and those in the normal department of the University increased from $28 to $75.[63] By March of 1907, there were the following types of schools on the island:[64]

Type	Number	Pupils enrolled
Graded Schools	528	22,870
Rural Schools	623	28,970
High Schools	3	155
Industrial schools	3	231
Normal School	1	123
Agricultural School	1	26
Night Schools	74	2,646
Total private schools	184	5,302
Total public schools	1233	54,985

Total number of teachers employed
          private schools   39
          public schools   1175

The figures show an increase of nearly 4,000 pupils over the enrollment of the preceeding year. The interest in educational matters is demonstrated by the considerable number of students who were sent to the United States to receive an education. In 1907. 492 pupils were studying in the United States, 141 of these were in colleges and universities, and the others were in secondary and primary schools.[65]

Only young women who had graduated near the top of their high school classes, or with honors from the normal school were eligible for a scholarship to study in the United States: each had to agree to return to the island and devote four years to public school service. In 1908 the value of the scholarship was raised from $400 to $500 a year. In that year, there were 25 scholarships for men and 14 for women.[66]

With the emphasis on improving the quality of education, graduations were special occasions. In 1907, ceremony for Central High School was held in the Ateneo Puertorriqueño. Governor Post presented the diplomas and the Insular Police Band played musical selections. The first Commissioner to the United States Congress, Federico Degetau, gave the address. There were eighteen graduates.[67]

In his Report of 1909 the Governor mentioned the great interest the teachers had shown in presenting school programs, so much so that it was difficult for him to decide to whom the diploma of excellence should be awarded that year.[68] He referred to an elaborate concert that took place on the evening of Thanksgiving Day, and another performance in Juncos. The exercises in Humacao surpassed anything he had seen at a school fiesta. The program began with a court scene, with a king and queen representing the Spanish royalty seated on a throne. After various speeches had been made by members of the court, Uncle Sam made his appearance accompanied by Columbia and attendants. They presented "Education," as represented by books and other objects, to the king and queen.

In Arecibo on Washington's Birthday there was an elaborate fiesta in the opera house in the evening, and in San Juan on the Fourth of July the children, about 1,000 in number, costumed in red, white, and blue, marched through the streets in the form of a long pennant about 300 feet long. In the place directly in front of the reviewing stand, upon which the Governor and other dignitaries sat, the pennant was changed into an American flag nearly 100 feet long. In this formation, the children sang America, the Star Spangled Banner, and other songs.[69]

A school festival was held in the Municipal Theatre in 1910, under the direction of Señoritas

Collins, Noell, and Field. The program was varied, consisting of drills, rhythm band selections, and dances. The children from the Lincoln School sang a chorus from a zarzuela, La Gran Vía, Lincoln School Kindergarten performed a minuet, San Juan No. 1 School performed a wand drill, a dumb bell drill, and a tambourine drill, and sang a selection from a zarzuela, A las máscaras.[70]

At the Normal School in Río Piedras programs were given featuring the music of Franz Joseph Haydn, with selections from his music. The Campos Choral Society sang The Emperor's Hymn and The Heaven's Are Telling from THE CREATION. They were assisted by Julián Andino (violin) and Franz Rooms (cello), well-known musicians of the day, playing selections such as Trio in G, with Miss Gilley, the director, playing the piano.[71] Their program in June featured the music of Beethoven and Schubert. After discussion of the lives of the composers and recitations about the music, Profesor Martínez Plée played the Kreutzer Violin Sonata and J. Sodring played the Sonata Pathetique for piano. The Campos Choral Society sang The Wanderer's Song and Serenade, Julio Toro sang Hedge Rose, and Rosario Salgado, Hark, Hark the Lark.[72]

Music was always included in programs of special observances for holidays and public functions which also included the finest island musicians. Teachers Conferences were held on the island and continued the tradition stated a decade earlier to educate the island natives. Informative talks were made by leading civic personalities, well-educated political figures, and educators and students continued to be sent to the United States to continue their education.

NOTES

1. United States Senate Document 3875, 56th Congress, Vol. 33. Document No. 363, p. 82.

2. Ibid.

3. United States Senate Document, 60th Congress, No. 5393, pp. 220-221.

4. María M. Brau. Island in the Crossroad: The History of Puerto Rico. Garden City, N.Y.: Doubleday Zenith Books, 1968, p. 81. The SJN, IV/23 (January 16, 1900), 1, gave the story that the first American school was erected in Puerto Rico. The flag fluttered in the breeze. Children recited the Pledge to the flag and sang the Star Spangled Banner and Columbia the Gem of the Ocean. There were 350 pupils, eight teachers, and one principal.

5. United States Senate Document, 60th Congress, No. 5393, p. 219.

6. The New York Times, XLIX (December 18, 1899), 6.

7. Brau, p. 83.

8. United States Senate Document 3875, 56th Congress, Vol. 33, Document 363, p. 26.

9. The New York Times, (April 1, 1899), 8.

10. SJN, IV/5 (January 5, 1900), 1.

11. Ibid., IV/23 (January 16, 1900), 1.

12. Ibid., IV/263 (June 15, 1900),1.

13. Ibid., V/81 (October 8, 1900), 1.

14. Ibid., V/75 (September 28, 1900), 1.

15. María Luisa Muñoz, "La educación musical en Puerto Rico," Educación, XIII/10 (November, 1963), 108.

16. Robert M. Fitzmaurice. Music Education in Puerto Rico: A Historical Survey with Guidelines for an Exemplary Curriculum. Tallahassee, Florida: Florida State University Ph.D. dissertation, 1970, p. 138.

17. Callejo, p. 71.

18. Fitzmaurice, p. 142.

19. Muñoz, p. 108.

20. United States Senate Document 3875, pp. 181-185.

21. SJN, IV/57 (February 4, 1900), 1.

22. Ibid., IV/85 (February 22, 1900), 2.

23. Ibid., IV/79 (February 18, 1900), 1.

24. Ibid., IV/57 (February 4, 1900), 1.

25. Ibid., IV/91 (February 27, 1900), 1.

26. Ibid., IV/275 (June 22, 1900), 1.

27. BM, LXIII/122 (May 27, 1901), 2.

28. SJN, VI/138 (June 14, 1901), 3.

29. Ibid., VI/140 (June 16, 1901), 3; VI/141 (June 17, 1901), 8, and VI/142 (June 19, 1901), 3.

30. LaC, (June 17, 1901), 2.

31. Course of Study and Duties of Teachers 1901-2. San Juan: Department of Education, San Juan News Press, 1901, pp. 8-14.

32. BM, LXIV/135 (June 12, 1902), 2, at Bus Stop 22.

33. Ibid., LXIV/147 (June 26, 1902), 2.

34. SJN, VII/369 (December 6, 1902), 8.

35. Ibid., VII/59 (March 11, 1902), 3.

36. United States Senate Document No. 3875, p. 83.

37. United States Senate Document No. 5393, p. 225.

38. SJN, VII/19 (January 23, 1902), 2.

39. Ibid., VIII/69 (March 25, 1903), 3.

40. Ibid., VIII/222 (September 29, 1903), 8.

41. Ibid., VIII/273 (November 26, 1903), 8.

42. Ibid., VIII/41 (February 20, 1903), 5.

43. Ibid., VIII/46 (February 27, 1903), 3.

44. Ibid., VIII/135 (June 13, 1903), 5.

45. Ibid.

46. BM, LXV/64 (March 18, 1903), 2.

47. Ibid., LXV/72 (March 27, 1903), 2, and LXV/70 (March 25, 1903), 2.

48. SJN, VIII/70 (March 26, 1903), 8, and VIII/73 (March 29, 1903), 3. According to ibid., VIII/69 (March 25, 1903), 3, in Ponce Miss Rossevelt and Governor Hunt would be guests of Carlos Armstrong. The reception to be given in her honor "will be the most brilliant one ever recorded in the history of the city."

49. BM, LXV/72 (March 27, 1903), 2.

50. SJN, VIII/71 (March 27, 1903), 1.

51. Ibid., VIII/73 (March 29, 1903), 1.

52. Fitzmaurice, p. 142.

53. SJN, VIII/265 (November 17, 1903), 8.

54. Ibid., VIII/278 (December 3, 1903), 7.

55. Ibid., VIII/279 (December 4, 1903), 4; VIII/280 (December 5, 1903), 1, and VIII/281 (December 6, 1903), 7.

56. A. Liebes, pp. 979-980.

57. United States Senate Document No. 5393, p. 228, in The Report of the Commissioner of Education. When the idea was first announced in the SJN, VIII/280 (December 5, 1903), 8, the teachers were told that Uncle Sam might pay the expenses.

58. SJN, IX/179 (August 6, 1904), 8.

59. United States Senate Document No. 5070, 56th Congress, 2nd Session, Document 135, p. 148.

60. BM, LXVIII/149 (June 26, 1906), 5.

61. United States Senate Document No. 5070, Document 135, p. 148.

62. Report of the Department of the Interior for the Fiscal Year Ended June 30, 1907, I. Washington, D.C.: Government Printing Office, 1908, Chapter IV, p. 362.

63. United States Senate Document No. 5393, p. 20.

64. Report of the Department of the Interior (1907), p. 366.

65. As early as 1900 pupils were encouraged to study in the United States. In the SJN, IV/108 (March 13, 1900), 1, Mr. Hoxthausen, "a well-known teacher," advertised that he would be going to the United States soon and "will take take charge of a son you desire to send to the United States to be educated." Apply 62 Sol Street.

66. United States Senate Document No. 5393, p. 201.

67. LaC, (June 20, 1907), 4.

68. United States Senate Document No. 5393, p. 207.

69. Ibid., and La Educación, I/11 (July 1, 1909), 14, stated that children marched accompanied by their respective teachers.

70. LaC, (May 24, 1910), 1.

71. Ibid., (May 10, 1910), 5.

72. Ibid., (June 17, 1910), 3.

CHAPTER VI

THE MUSICAL ACTIVITIES ON THE ISLAND

When Spain ceded sovereignty over Puerto Rico to the United States in 1898, Puerto Rico retained its Hispanic character and its Hispanic culture. Evidence shows that the musical culture did not decline. Musical activities continued on the island throughout the first decade of the era. Programs and contests continued as usual in the Ateneo Puertorriqueño; more musical bands were formed and weekly concerts were offered in the city parks. The solemn celebration of holy days continued, and instrumental ensembles still played for special church feast days. Some of the American officials took an active role in Puerto Rican cultural activities, as seen above. Most important of all, many Pueto Rican composers and performers were very active during this era, and the Ateneo Puertorriqueño was the scene of many musical programs.

1. THE ATENEO PUERTORRIQUEÑO

The Ateneo Puertorriqueño was founded in 1876, and it promoted the arts by encouraging the development of literary forms, musical compositions, musical performance, and the other fine arts. The theatrical life in Puerto Rico began at the Ateneo, which culminated with the festival of the Puerto Rican theatre under the auspices of the Instituto de Cultura Puertorriqueña. Since the famous "Ode to Puerto Rico" by José Gautier Benítez, which won in 1877, the first literary contest, it is difficult to find any native writer, artist, or musician of any importance who did not participate and succeed in the annual contests of this venerable institution. Tavárez, Morel Campos, and Braulio Dueño Colón, among others, were acclaimed at the Ateneo.

The Ateneo sponsored contests in 1882 to 1888, 1893, 1896-97, 1901, 1903, and 1906 to 1908. Analysis of the dates clearly indicate that the Ateneo's activities did not change in response to change in government.[1] In 1901 an award was given to José De Diego for his poem, Ante la historia. The contest of 1903 was announced for June 29th, the twenty-seventh anniversary of the founding of the Ateneo.[2]

According to The San Juan News, however, the contest was held in September.[3] After a speech by the newly-elected president, Manuel Fernández Juncos, the Insular Police Band played a fantasía from Carmen.[4] Awards were presented to several participants, including first prize to Cristobal Real and Ferdinand R. Cesteros, third prize to Ramón Negrón Flores, and honorable mention to José De Diego, Clemente Ramírez, Vicente Palés, Negrón Flores, and Cayetano Coll y Toste. Fernández Juncos also won a prize for the translation of a work by an American author. The Ateneo did not differentiate between the type of awards given to the participants.[5] The San Juan News called the "literary affair at the Ateneo a success." The evening opened with the Puerto Rico Regiment Band playing a symphony "in a masterly style," for which it received a "merited applause." Cecilia Bruno sang a Romanza composed by Fernando Callejo to a text by Clemente Ramírez de Arellano. "Bruno was an artist whose reputation is unparalleled in Puerto Rico," and the newspapers indicated that the new composition "will undoubtedly win much popularity among musicians and music lovers."[6] The prize in 1904 was won by Manuel Rodríguez Arreson, a Puerto Rican composer residing in Puerto Plata in the Dominican Republic. Juan Viñolo was awarded honorable mention. The judges were Anita Otero, Trinidad Padilla Sanz, and Braulio Dueño Colón.[7] In 1906 the only prize-winning medal was awarded to Ramón Negrón Flores.[8] A tribute was given to the director of the Ateneo in 1907. Augusto Malaret won the gold medal that year for his prize-winning biography of Manuel Fernández Juncos. During the ceremony the Insular Police Orchestra, under the direction of Francisco Verar, performed.[9]

The jury for the 1908 contest included Francisco Verar, Dueño Colón, Luis Miranda, and Justo Pastor Torres.[10] They awarded gold medals in the categories of literature, poetry, painting, and music. Rafael Balseiro Dávila won a gold medal and diploma of honor for his concert waltz, entitled Puerto Rico. A bronze medal was awarded to Monsita Ferrer Otero for her essay, La música es la lenguaje del ideal.[11] Although the Ateneo booklet did not list other music awards, according to the Boletín Mercantil de Puerto Rico, Juan Ríos Ovalle won a silver medal for his danza, Teresa.[12] Callejo also mentions a contest for 1909,[13] but according to the Records of the Ateneo, there were no contests from

1909 through 1912.[14] Prize winning compositions do not appear to have been preserved by the Ateneo, but there are tapes of recent concerts of significant works by a few of the composers, namely José Ignacio Quintón,[15] Braulio Dueño Colón,[16] and Jesús Figueroa Iriarte.[17]

According to the Records of the Board of Directors and Officers of the Ateneo, elections were held each year with the exception of 1899. Among those members of the Board during this era were Federico Degetau, in 1900 and 1908. George Cabot Ward was elected on December 28, 1908 for the next year, and Martín Travieso and Rafael Balseiro were elected on December 21, 1909 for the next year. On December 28, 1910, Luis Miranda was elected to serve in 1911.

A 1903 editorial in The San Juan News reflected on the Ateneo as a cultural center.[18] It shows the attitude toward this institution, and bears repetition here:

> "On this occasion there had gathered together representatives of the best families of the island and the best literary talent to assist in the ceremonies . . . .
>
> Like most institutions of its kind, its existence has been a more or less checkered one. At times it had ridden the wave crests of prosperity and on other occasions it had dragged itself along the sands of adversity, glad to be able to exist at all. In fact, subsequent to the American occupation, its existence was a problem and but for the assistance rendered it by a few liberal hearted members, it is an open question whether it would be in existence today.
>
> The Puerto Ricans, like the great majority of the Latin races, are poetic, artistic, sentimental in their natures, and these traits of character are such as deserve to be cultivated and nurtured, for the reason that they serve to develop the finer instincts of our human race.
>
> The Atheneum should be in the future as it has been in the past . . . . where its members are all working for the one common

purpose of developing and enobling the Puerto Rican character."

Throughout the decade the Ateneo was used for a variety of occasions such as receptions, recitals of pupils of the members, concerts to celebrate the feast of Saint Cecilia, and benefit programs.

2. THE MUSIC IN THE CHURCHES

In the Puerto Rican churches of the early twentieth century, Gregorian Chant as well as choir music accompanied by instrumental ensembles existed. The style of choral performance did not change--each church continued to have its organist who taught the various songs and chants.[1] In the churches of Old San Juan both Ratisbon and Solesmes editions of the chant were found by this author. In addition, manuscripts scored for orchestral ensembles can be located in churches, private collections, and in the Archivo General de Puerto Rico. It is evident that most of the earlier mentioned composers wrote for choir and orchestra, indicating that large ensembles continued to participate in church services and events. Even in cases where only one copy for one instrument can be located, the title usually indicates that an instrumental ensemble was to accompany the voices. Manuscripts dated during this period illustrate that there was an attempt to continue the tradition that was prevalent on the island in the nineteenth century.

In 1973, this author found in Puerto Rican churches musical compositions which were performed during the time period under study. They were discovered in the San Juan Cathedral choir loft, in the Churches of San José and San Francisco, all in Old San Juan, and others were deposited in the Archivo General de Puerto Rico. San Francisco Church always had a choir and orchestra for special feasts, and there was a great deal of sheet music in its choir library. Of the other two churches visited, Saint Ann's Church in Old San Juan had no music, and the chapel at the Hospital de la Concepción (Sisters of the Servants of Mary) had only contemporary church music with Spanish texts, a Gregorian mass (1965), and several copies of a hymn book published in Spain (1970).[2]

The Morlá private collection in Hato Rey contained the music of Ramón Morlá Trenchs (1875-1953). It includes manuscript and published church music for band, orchestra, string quartet, religious as well as secular songs, piano music, choruses, and zarzuelas. Among the church music are hymns, masses, litanies, gozos, salves, and a requiem. Many of the pieces are scored for orchestra, but few are dated. Morlá arrived in Puerto Rico in 1896 and subsequently held many important church organist positions, including that at the San Juan Cathedral (1926-1940). He is most important for this study as his work shows that the nineteenth century tradition was carried on into the twentieth century. His music will be discussed in Chapter VII.

3. THE CELEBRATION OF HOLY DAYS

Along with the American holidays, the Puerto Ricans celebrated many religious holy days. According to a specialist in Puerto Rican cultural history, in 1898 Puerto Ricans stopped celebrating Spanish feast days and began celebrating the "fiestas" of the United States. However, they continued to celebrate the Patron Saints' feasts and other traditional festivals.[1]

The religious influence of Spain remained, and it has an important influence on the island even today. Each town has a Patron Saint and each Saint has a special day on the calendar. The Patron Saint fiestas are celebrated with various activities, including contests, concerts, dances, exhibitions, games, novenas, and solemn masses. Festivities last approximately two weeks around the Patron Saint calendar day. Of course, in addition to the Patron Saints of the towns, the Saint's days are celebrated by the churches named for those Saints, and there are additional celebrations for certain Saints, solemnized with masses including vocal and instrumental music. The feast of San Rafael was always celebrated with an instrumental ensemble performing during the mass in the Church of San Francisco, Old San Juan.

The Christmas season is a special time of celebrating in Puerto Rico. The season begins on December 16.[2] There are nine days of daily mass in

82

all of the Catholic Churches in the morning--<u>Misa de aguinaldo</u>, named for the music that is played during the service. After the Christmas Eve Mass, <u>Misa de gallo</u>, there is a roast pig feast attended by the immediate members of each family, followed by dancing and singing of Christmas carols.

Many small towns in Puerto Rico have casinos, where dances are frequently held and where balls are held two or three times a year--one is usually on New Year's Eve. January festivities culminate with the celebration of the Three Kings' Day, one for each Magi. Although a visitor to San Juan between Christmas and January 6 will find it nearly impossible to accomplish any work, it is an excellent time to participate in island activities and learn more about the culture and the people.

It was the same in the early part of the twentieth century. In January of 1903, for example, the town of Toja Baja was finally back to normal. According to <u>The San Juan News</u>, from December 16 to the 11th of January the town had been the scene of constant merrymaking. There were <u>misas de aguinaldos</u>, and military drills, and Professor Andrés Rodríguez's band played after a calisthenics drill and again that night for a "great dance" in Constancia.[3]

On September 8, 1903, there was a celebration of the feast of Our Lady of Monserrate. The stores were closed for the greater part of the day. In the evening there was a ball in the casino, "which was attended by the best elements of San Juan Society."[4] There was also entertainment during the evening in private residences throughout the region.

Stores were closed and speeches were made on the feast days. Bands performed in the streets and there were great balls at night. Major feast days, such as December 8, the feast of the Immaculate Conception, were preceded by a nine day novena, during which there were fireworks at 5 a.m. and festivities were held throughout the day. Gifts would be distributed to the poor. Very often there was a concert in the evening--especially on November 22, Saint Cecilia's Day. Instrumental ensembles accompanied the church services on those special days.

Sometimes the celebrations were a little too festive, with too much merrymaking. Such was the case back in August of 1899 after the feast of the Assumption on the plantation in Vieques Isle. It was customary on this day to give all of the working men a holiday, along with all the rum they could drink. When they were filled with rum, the laborers proceeded to take possession of the island and after fighting among themselves and terrorizing the citizens, the riot had to be supressed by the Insular Police, who had to kill one man and wound another before order was restored.[5]

Usually in the afternoon of the day of the Patron Saint's feast, there would be a ball for the children. During the fiestas there were sometimes comical scenes worth repeating: for example, in 1901, a quartet of mandolin and guitar players, which included some of the well-known young businessmen of San Juan, serenaded several señoritas. Under one balcony they were showered with roses and jasmines; at another house, however, a well-aimed bucket of water ended the serenade--the quartet returned home for a change of clothes.[6]

By 1906, some Puerto Ricans felt that their traditional feasts were suffering in the light of the celebrations of American holidays. They insisted that the feast of their Island Patron Saint should remain a local celebration and not be linked to any United States holiday such as the Fourth of July. The editor of The San Juan News expressed his enthusiasm for this old celebration. In analyzing its significance, he stated that

> "The people of Puerto Rico recognize it fully. It is not a religious occasion, not a church festival; it is a Puerto Rican tradition, one that symbolizes the personality of this people; it is a patriotic and time honored observance which ought to be celebrated by all those who lost their country; for it represents and constitutes something that is the soul and personality of a people."[7]

Pleased by the widespread interest in a more solemn and more splendid celebration that year, the editor concluded his next editorial with the following remarks:

"A people which defends its traditions --which are its past glories--and find in them the strength which they need to fearlessly and serenely face the future, are deserving of respect. Those who cannot share our enthusiasm, who cannot feel what we feel because of the change that has come to our people, ought at least to respect this sublime moment in which a people unite in order to fulfill their lofty destiny and the inscrutable designs of History and of God."[8]

When their festivities were over and their brilliant success was sung, the editor chided those Puerto Ricans who neither contributed nor partook in their festivities. Apparently those who refused to help or contribute toward the success of the celebration criticized the efforts of others. The editor's final editorial ended in the following manner:

"It is both sad and ridiculous for those weak and vacillating individuals, who have no patriotism nor respect for tradition, to attempt to disparage and discredit the work done by others who have exercised their faculties and initiative in defense of useful and cherished ideals; we advise all such to cease their insensate efforts of blind obstruction, which are unwise as well as suicidal.

Patriotism, regard for tradition and attention to something that has been sanctioned by the highest Puertorrican representation, ought to have commanded respect . . . . The feast of San Juan is not one that has been disinterred from among the dead traditions but one that has actual life and that was confirmed by the representative body of Puerto Ricans on a recent occasion which is recalled by every one."[9]

BANDS THAT ENTERTAINED ON THE ISLAND OF PUERTO RICO

1898-1910

	1898	1899	1900	1901	1902	1903	1904	1905	1906	1907	1908	1909	1910
Borínquen Band / La Banda Puertorriqueña		X	X	X									
Boys' Charity School Band			X	X	X	X	X	X	X	X	X	X	X
Bomberos--San Juan / Ponce		X	X	X	X	X	X	X	X	X	X	X	X
Sixth U.S. Infantry			X										
Cantá Lafayette		X											
Eleventh Infantry	X	X	X										
Fifth Cavalry			X										
Fifty-sixth Regiment						X							
Juventud del Comercio						X	X	X					
Nineteenth Regiment		X											
Insular Police Band				X	X	X	X	X	X	X	X	X	X
Banda del Batallón / Regiment de Puerto Rico			X	X	X	X	X	X	X		X	X	X

4. THE BAND CONCERTS IN THE CITY PARKS

During the decade following the Spanish American War, the old tradition of band concerts in the city parks continued. At least twelve bands were active on the island.[1] (See chart on opposite page.) In addition to regularly scheduled concerts, there were occasional holiday festivities with more than one band participating. Typical band programs for 1898 through 1910 included selections from zarzuelas and operas, danzas by Morel Campos, Tavárez, and other popular musicians of their day, and by the band directors themselves, and music by European composers. In the early part of the century, American patriotic songs were included in the programs.

Some bands were in existence during the entire time period, while others soon disappeared. Among the latter were bands connected with military units or with pleasure or cruise ships that stopped at the port of San Juan. Of the United States military units, the Fifth Cavalry, Sixth and Eleventh Infantries, Navy and Marine Bands entertained while they were stationed on the island. On one memorable occasion, the Marine Band attached to the U.S.S. Buffalo gave a surprise concert in the Plaza on a Saturday evening. It was reported that everyone in the vicinity enjoyed the "rare treat, . . . the best concert they had heard all winter."[2] Some of the units had drum and bugle corps, and the Fifth Cavalry had a band mounted on white horses.[3] These groups performed on religious holidays, for musicals and with other island bands at civic ceremonies.

In 1898 and 1899 there were advertisements in the newspapers announcing band concerts but neither programs nor the names of the band and its director were given. As early as January, 1899, a musical band from the Lafayette Quarters played in Ponce,[4] the Nineteenth Regiment Band played for a fiesta of the "Sociedad Patriótica Puertorriqueña,"[5] and a military band provided music for a religious occasion.[6]

A Puerto Rican Firemen's Band was also performing as early as 1899 when it played in the Plaza.[7] It also performed occasionally early in 1900 and gave regular concerts on Sunday evenings during the summer months.[8] On Memorial Day in Mayagüez in 1901, the

Firemen's Band accompanied 200 voices singing <u>America</u> and the <u>Star Spangled Banner</u>.[9] In October the Ponce Fireman's Band directed by Domingo Cruz gave concerts on two Sunday evenings,[10] and at the end of the year gave a concert in the Plaza.[11] Programs included music by Verdi and Morel Campos, as well as other lesser-known composers.

Especially prominent among the early bands on the island was the Eleventh U.S. Infantry Band which arrived in Puerto Rico on August 1, 1898,[12] and was very active through 1900. Under the direction of Stephen Jelinek, it played for dances, balls, programs commemorating patriotic holidays, and at benefit concerts.[13] A typical concert included an overture, selection from a zarzuela, a military drill with musical accompaniment, instrumental solos, quartets (officers with well-known local musicians), and solos by local singers such as Cecilia Bruno. The band had a fine reputation and always received fine reviews. At one benefit program, Major Stevens and Miss Davis sang <u>Oh That We Two Were Maying</u>, and a reviewer declared that they were "charming," that Davis sang a solo with such a powerful voice that she "held the audience spellbound," and that "the band was never better in tune, each musician winding his part like a faithful clock, never striking before the hour."[14]

The band performed at open air concerts at its barracks every Friday night for the officers and their friends.[15] The popularity of the band was apparent from an article that appeared in March of 1900, inquiring, "If the 11th Infantry Band should play in the Plaza this evening, could the Plaza hold all the people attracted there?"[16] The Eleventh Infantry Band joined other bands on special occasions; when Governor Allen returned to the island, for instance, it played at a reception on the wharf.[17] It also played at special parties like the lawn party at Casa Blanca,[18] and a Yacht Club Ball,[19] and they performed in the Plaza for the Fourth of July celebration.[20]

The weekly concerts of the Eleventh Infantry Band featured music by Jelinek himself, as well as by Auber, Donizetti, Flotow, Gounod, Rossini, Sousa, Strauss, Thomas, William Vincent Wallace, and lesser-known composers.[21] Although they received their orders to return to the United States in July, the band was active on the island until the first of December.[22] During this time, newspapers continued to promote a possible concert by them in the Plaza but to no avail.[23] When Stephen Jelinek left for Newport News, Virginia, with his band and the entire Eleventh Infantry, they were serenaded from the dock by the Puerto Rico Regiment Band with Dixie, the Star Spangled Banner, Rally Round the Flag, Boys, Home Sweet Home, and Yankee Doodle.[24]

There were during this time, four outstanding Puerto Rican band directors--Francisco Verar, of the Puerto Rican Band and later the Insular Police Band, Luis R. Miranda of the Regiment of Puerto Rico Band, Juan Viñolo of the Boys' Charity School Band, and Manuel Tizol of the Juventud del Comercio Band. Verar, who had been associated with bands ever since he was seventeen years old (1867), directed the weekly concerts of La Banda Puertorriqueña in the Plaza de Armas, Old San Juan. Its programs give one an opportunity to assess not only its contribution but also the height of musical culture of that time. The only record found of his directing in 1898 was in the Report of the Auditor of Puerto Rico to the 56th Congress (1900) which stated that Francisco Verar Marcano was paid $66 for material furnished for the concert at the orphan asylum in October of 1898.[25] In August, 1899, his band gave concerts on Wednesdays and Sundays from 7 to 8 p.m.[26] Music performed at his band concerts during 1899 included selections from many well-known operas and zarzuelas, as well as danzas by Puerto Rican composers: Mislán, Morel Campos, Tavárez, Pasarell, and Viñolo.

Verar's organization was active again in 1900, when it performed on January 31 to "fully 2000 people in the plaza." The program was "exceptionally good," and many encores were called for. The chief attraction was Surrender of Santiago, which was accompanied by "redfire and rockets."[27] Verar's fifteen piece band played for the "White Bow and Arrow Club" dances in the Theatre,[28] performed in the plaza during the carnival season,[29] and on Wednesday nights through June when the programs had to be suspended because of lack of funds.[30]

La Banda Puertorriqueña participated in a benefit concert for the Maternity Hospital sponsored by the Ladies Aid Society and played at the Yacht Club Ball for the Fourth of July.[31] In San Juan, on July

15th, the second anniversary of the American Occupation, the Puerto Rico Band paraded through the streets at 5:30 a.m. playing patriotic songs and later, at 8 p.m. in Plaza Alfonso XII. Verar and the band played Spanish and Puerto Rican songs, including La Borinqueña. From August through December 1900, Verar's band played one concert each week. Programs included Puerto Rican danzas, opera selections, dance music and band music. He also organized an instrumental ensemble in order to perform orchestral music for public and private functions.

The Puerto Rican Band went on strike in January, 1901, and does not appear to have given concerts until March when it resumed its weekly concerts. Programs included works by Andino, Caballero, Morel Campos, Chapi, Donizetti, Duchesne, Madera, Sousa, Suppé, Tavárez, Tizol, Verdi, and Wagner.[32] It considered attending the Buffalo Exposition and asked for $2 a day for their expenses.[33] Their June concert included works by Agrinzony, Valverde, Hamilton, and the usual well-known composers.[34] Because of lack of funds, they played only two more concerts and marched in the Fourth of July parade.[35] It was a "glorious Fourth; celebrated in a truly American style . . . . "[36] Its final concert on July 14 concluded with Patria by Dueño Colón and La Borinqueña.[37]

During this time, an Insular Police Corps composed entirely of Puerto Ricans, with the exception of the Chief and Assistant Chief, was organized under the direction of Major General Guy B. Henry, Governor.[38] Now that the Puerto Rican Band was unable to be funded, it was converted into the Insular Police Band. In September, an advertisement appeared in the newspaper for recruits for the Police Band. Only applicants who had a knowledge of music were invited to apply, and entrance examinations were administered.[39] Three people applied for the post as Director and Francisco Verar was appointed band leader.[40] Verar had eighteen years experience as a leader of various military bands and he held the rank of Second Lieutenant in the Insular Police. His salary was $75 a month.[41] By September 14, the announcement was made that the band was complete with fourteen members, with a projected twenty-four.[42] According to La Democracia, there were twenty-four by the end of September and eventually there would be thirty-five.[43]

90

A fund was created out of the monies received by the police for playing at various private parties as a band, in small ensembles, or as an orchestra. They used the funds to purchase music, repair instruments, and meet band expenses that could not easily be met from the regular police appropriation. In the records of the United States Congress, it was suggested that the money be placed in an insular treasury as a trust fund, or put directly in the charge of the Chief.[44]

The Insular Police Band was inaugurated on October 15th. The San Juan News had great praise for it and stated that Professor Verar was highly satisfied with the musicians.[45] They progressed so well that they serenaded Governor Hunt on October 14, the last day of official mourning for President McKinley.[46] The program featured the danza Patria by Dueño Colón, a two-step Insular Police by Verar, and other works. There were twenty-four musicians now and the members of the band were on duty all the time at the Executive Mansion. They were organized as a band for the Governor to have at command on occasions such as public receptions. While the "Mayflower" was in port, the ship's band was used for public receptions, and at other times the military bands were used. Since the military were not always in San Juan, it was thought best to organize the police band.[47]

The band apparently played very well because the type of music changed to selections by well-known composers, especially arrangements from operas --Sonnanbula, Tannhaüser, the Barber of Seville, and Bohemian Girl. Verar was featured as a clarinet soloist with the band,[48] and the band delighted the promenaders in the Plaza with concerts even on Christmas night.[49]

In 1902 it played regular concerts in the Plaza featuring the same type of band music along with Irish airs, but in March presented a new program that included Hungarian Rhapsody No. 2 by Liszt, and a march dedicated to the President of Cuba, Estrada Palma. Nearly every number was encored.[50] For a special Saint Patrick's Day celebration at the Governor's Palace it added Wearing of the Green, as requested by the Governor.[51] The selections on their programs now included more music by Puerto Rican composers--El Patateo by Verar, Chief Techter

91

March by Viñolo, _Idilio_ by Morel Campos, Simón
Madera's danza _Lejos de Tí_,[52] _Aires del País_,
Chorreao, and _El Jíbaro_ by Andino,[53] _Los
Golondrinas_ by Braulio Dueño Colón, and _Mis Pesares_
by Agrinzony;[54] and more selections from
operas--_Grand March_ by Meyerbeer, _Cavalleria
Rusticana_ by Mascagni, and _Dei Freischütz_ by Weber.

It performed at a Teachers Conference, at the
Ateneo Puertorriqueño, and at a reception at the
"Pink Palace" (3 Fortaleza Street) which was
reportedly "the swellest social affair of the
season."[55] It played at a reception for the
Governor's daughter the evening before she left for
the United States,[56] and at the dedication of the
normal school in Río Piedras where they accompanied
the school chorus directed by Stella Test.[57] On the
Fourth of July concert it featured soloists Teresina
Moreno Calderón who sang _Hail Columbia_, and Cecilia
Bruno who sang _Columbia the Gem of the Ocean_.[58]
When the Puerto Rico Regiment left for Cayey, the
editor of _The San Juan News_ inquired if Verar and his
band might start performing twice a week.[59] At the
request of the Mayor, Acting Governor Hartzell
instructed the band to give a concert in the Plaza on
July 25th because it was a holiday,[60] and during
August they performed at weekly concerts in the
Plaza. At the end of the month it received new
selections for the coming concerts, musical
attachments for the instruments, as well as materials
for uniforms so that all would be dressed alike.[61]
In September the Acting Governor ordered them to play
in Plaza Colón on Saturday night and to continue in
the Plaza Principal on Wednesday nights.[62]

The band accompanied a chorus during a benefit
for Teresina Moreno Calderón so that she might finish
her musical education in the United States. The
program was sponsored by the Ladies Aid Society.
Admission was $5 (Box), $1 (Orchestra, 50 cents
(General Admission), 15 cents (Balcony), and choice
seats in the balcony were 20 cents.[63] When Governor
Hunt and his family returned to Puerto Rico, the
Police Band gave a delightful program throughout the
evening.[64] They performed in various cities and
towns on the island throughout the year, played
German music for the German soldiers who were in
port,[65] and presented "genuine" Puerto Rican and
Spanish music during a concert in December.[66] The
last program was under the direction of Casimiro

Duchesne who also directed the string orchestra of the Police Band during an Arbor Day program at the Lincoln School.[67] The band played a benefit for the San Juan Graded High School in the Municipal Theatre to raise money for library books,[68] and ended the year playing a New Year's Eve program which included Paderewski's Minuet under the direction of Verar in the Plaza.[69]

In 1903, the Police Band had a busy schedule from early January until the end of December. It began the year playing in Coamo for the farewell to the Chief of Police, Frank Techter, who cried as Home, Sweet Home was played.[70] The Secretary's Register of Puerto Rico for 1903 stated, "The Insular Police Band composed of members of the force, is an organization of superior merit and is very popular with the people."[71] By this time it was giving three concerts a week,[72] and was scheduled to play at the Saint Louis Exposition, where "It would be an object lesson to all who might have the fortune to hear them play. It would give the visitors to the exposition a better idea of the artistic and musical temperament of our people than all the newspaper articles that could possibly be written."[73]

The weekly concerts of the Police Band usually included seven numbers plus the Star Spangled Banner. 1903 was a successful year for the band and in a letter from Louis Sutzbacher in The San Juan News, Verar was complimented on his clarinet solo which "was very fine and impressed me favorably. In the short time the band has been under your leadership it has made wonderful progress. You deserve great praise, and fame as a band leader."[74]

In 1904 the Insular Police Band was by far the busiest musical organization of all the groups performing for the public. From January to December it was now playing concerts on Thursday and Saturday evenings, Sunday afternoons, and regularly entertaining the guests at the Governor's mansion. It always included danzas by Puerto Rican composers, very often two or three at one concert. When the band played for a benefit in the Theatre in late January, it received high praise from the press as "a grand institution improving every day. There are few bands anywhere in the country more thoroughly equipped with talent and ability to furnish good music."[75]

93

February and March included the usual concerts in the parks for audiences of tourists who were "out in full force" and apparently enjoyed the music.[76] There was a reception in the Governor's mansion,[77] and the band's Holy Week concert in the Plaza included the Ave Maria by Gounod, Stabat Mater by Rossini, Funeral March by Milpager, a work by Mendelssohn, and Funeral March and Lament from the opera Jones, ending with the Star Spangled Banner.[78] Their April programs presented several new Puerto Rican pieces: Marcha triunfal, América by Aristides Chavier, Si me quisieres by Morel Campos, Lluvia de perlas by Ríos Ovalle, Ideal by Jaime Pericas, and Fantasía militas Venezolana by Pedro Arcilagos.[79]

During a charity event in May, the Police Band and Boys' Charity School Band performed a work, Nita Gitana, by Reginald DeKoven,[80] and danzas, Candorosa by Morel Campos, and Tú y Yo by Angel Mislán.[81] In June three new members joined the Police Band: Mateo Cara Bulso, Pedro J. Oller, and Antonio Gandía,[82] and the group gave several concerts in the Casino and Plaza Delicias in Ponce. The news editor commented: "Never since the fair of 1882 has such a tremendous crowd of people gathered in our fashionable walk."[83] The band returned to San Juan on the 25th to give a grand send-off at the marina to the teachers sailing on U.S. transports to study in the States.[84] It participated in a memorable program at the Ateneo the last of June during which Amalia Paoli sang A Night in Venice and Federico Degetau gave a speech that "crowned the fiesta."[85]

In July during the inauguration ceremonies in the Municipal Theatre, the Police Band played Hail to the Chief for the new Governor, the Honorable Beekman Winthrop.[86] In July, danzas La Criolla by Dueño Colón and Mi Adorado by Ríos Ovalle were included with music by Flotow, Sousa, Thomas, Verdi, Valverde, and Waldteufel.[87] In August the band played at a reception given by Governor and Mrs. Winthrop for the teachers who returned from the states.[88] Plaza concerts included music by Escobes, Jiménez, Donizetti, Rossini, Tobani, Weber, Paul, Suppé, Sousa,[89] and danzas Se Acabó el Melao by Pasarell, and Lluvia de Perlas by Ríos Ovalle.[90]

Throughout his performance career, Francisco

Verar, director of the band was often praised for his artistic clarinet playing as he was after having played a solo during a concert in Plaza Baldorioty in September. That month the band played the usual concerts in the parks as well as at a reception hosted by the Governor and his family at Santa Catalina. A few new composer's names appeared on concert programs: Elembert, Sendra, Prediville, Barron, Hill, Clarke, and Mozart.[91]

November 22nd, the feast of Saint Cecilia Patron of Music, always featured a grand concert in the Theatre. The Police Band played under Verar's direction, Elisa Tavárez played a waltz for piano by Moskowski, Amalia Paoli sang Ave Maria from Otello by Verdi, and Cecilia Bruno and Amalia Paoli sang a duet, A Night in Venice.[92] Their programs in December included zarzuela selections, music from the 4th act of Il Trovatore, a pot-pourri of Puerto Rican airs, Navidad and Ecos de mi tierra by Dueño Colón, and works by Llado, Caballero, Recher, Restarfe, and Donizetti.[93]

During 1905, the Police Band kept up its busy schedule performing at Plaza Baldorioty, for a graduation ceremony, giving concerts in Borínquen Park, a July concert in the Presbyterian Church,[94] serenades at the Governor's mansion, a concert in Guayama which included playing for dancing in the Casino Español,[95] a celebration for patriot, Román Baldorioty de Castro,[96] played for Novena services in honor of the Immaculate Conception in San Francisco Church (November 28th to December 8th),[97] a memorial service in the Ateneo,[98] a reception at the Lincoln School,[99] and ended the year playing for a ball in the Union Club in Santurce.[100]

Music by Puerto Rican composers performed this year included the following pieces:

Danza, Pobre Borínquen, by Angel Mislán[101]

Danza, Ten Piedad, by Juan Morel Campos[102]

Tema Atenas by Ríos Ovalle[103]

Two-step, Good Bye, by Agrinzony[104]

Danza, Perlas de mi Patria, by Morel Campos[105]

95

Danza, Rosa María, by Ríos Ovalle[106]

Danza, Amor Bendito, by Ríos Ovalle [107]

Yankee Doodle by Colian[108]

La Polka de Ruiseñor with flute obligato by Dueño
    Colón[109]

Danza, Sueño de amor, by Morel Campos[110]

Danza, Ofelia, by Thomas Ponce[111]

Danza, Cuando me miro en tus ojos, by Julián
    Andino[112]

Danza, La bella Margot, by Morel Campos[113]

Sara, variaciones de Bombardino, by Angel
    Mislán[114]

Two-step, Colonel Hamill, by Viñolo[115]

Danza, Noche de verano, by José Ignacio
    Quintón[116]

Vals, El Pitirre, by Dueño Colón[117]

Danza, Volveré, by Cruz Verar[118]

Danza, Angelina, by Ríos Ovalle[119]

Danza, La Navidad, by Braulio Dueño Colón[120]

Pot-pourri Puertorriqueños by Morel Campos[121]

In 1906, the Police Band was often sent to cities by the Governor to participate in parades. It continued to perform at receptions in the executive mansion and at such special programs as the laying of the corner stone at the Colegio Sagrado Corazón,[122] a farewell reception at the harbor for Bishop Blenk in June,[123] and a reception at the executive mansion for Secretary of State Elihu Root.[124]

5. THE PUERTO RICO REGIMENT BAND

Another group, the Puerto Rico Regiment of the United States Fifth Infantry, was organized as a single battalion in March, 1899.[1] In 1900, another battalion was added, and a regimental organization, including a band, was formed. The regiment included 548 Puerto Rican soldiers and 31 officers, 8 of whom were citizens of Puerto Rico. The organizer of the Regiment was Colonel James A. Buchanan, later Brigadier General in the United States Army.

Justo de la Paz was placed in charge of the band on February 10, 1900, and all men detailed on special duty with the band reported to him.[2] By February 12, the battalion band began daily practice from 10 a.m. to 11 a.m. each day, with the exception of Sunday. Private Federico Verea was promoted to Corporal on February 13, and soon after he replaced de la Paz as head of the band of Company A.[3] Other musicians assigned to Cavalry Battalion, Company A, were trumpeters Francisco Pastrana, Rafael Niebes, Antonio Rodríguez, and Antonio Quirogas.[4] A new recruit, Benigni Affigni, assigned to Company D of the Battalion, U.S. V, was detailed to the band.[5] In April, Privates Manuel Carvava and José Calderi were assigned to the band,[6] and by late April the band performed the Puerto Rican hymn, La Borinqueña during a ceremony at which four of its companies and 75 members of the Insular Police were present.[7] In May, it joined the city bands in the playing of La Borinqueña and "all the people sang the tune so dear to their hearts."[8] Other selections they performed were by Boeltzer, Tobani, Miller, Alstine, and Sousa's High School Cadet's March.[9]

In May, they practiced every day from 7 to 8 a.m. and 10 to 11 a.m. with the exception of Saturday and Sunday by order of Lieutenant Colonel Buchanan.[10] Under Justo de la Paz, selections by the band included works by Groton, Beyer, del Oror, Duchesne, Gilbert and Sullivan, and Navarro. The band had been stationed in San Juan and in June was ordered to Cayey.[11] In August it played concerts every Tuesday evening at the barracks,[12] and an occasional program in the Plaza.[13]

In the fall of the year, Lieutenant Buchanan

appointed Corporal Luis R. Miranda of Company H of the Regiment to fill the existing vacancy.[14] Miranda first appeared in the records of the Regiment in 1900, when a uniform was issued to him in Ponce, Puerto Rico, on September 1. He was listed as a Corporal (in The U.S. Volunteer--Puerto Rico Regiment Papers in the United States National Archives [Washington, D.C.] #291, Orders 753.) Others with him at the Henry Barracks at that time who received uniforms were Private Ortiz, Mateo Cora, Justo de la Paz, Livio Villanueva, José Montilla, Francisco Pastrana, Ramiro Cruzado, Osvaldo Segarra, and Modesto Fernández. Their uniforms consisted of a "blue blouse, braided down front and around bottom, straight braided collar," and a regular "blue blouse."[15]

Corporal Luis Miranda, upon recommendation of the Company Commander, was promoted to Sergeant on October 10, 1900.[16] He next appears in the news when he conducted the band of the Puerto Rico Regiment in late October when Governor Allen visited Ponce.[17] According to The San Juan News, in December the Regiment Band awaited an invitation from the city to play in the Plaza. The announcement stated that the band had improved since its stay in Cayey, that it sounded as good as the Eleventh Infantry Band.[18] The reporter for The San Juan News suggested that the Puerto Rico Regiment Band might play alternately with the Puerto Rican Band because there was such a long wait between numbers.[19] In spite of this, the concerts were well attended.

The Regiment Band performed La Borinqueña on the docks as the Executive Council and House Delegates saw Governor Davis off on his trip to the States.[20] Their concert late in December included works by Suppé, Tobani, and others ending with a Mexican danza, María. by Dávila, and the national hymn. The concert received high praise and "far excelled any given there since the Eleventh Infantry Band discontinued playing there over 18 months ago . . . . every number was enthusiastically encored," and Professor Verea received deserving praise for his work in drilling the band.[21]

This band, also known as the Banda del Batallón de Puerto Rico, was quite active in 1901. It began offering concerts every Friday evening in the Plaza in San Juan when the Borínquen Band went on strike because the City Council cut their salaries from $90 to $50 a month for the 24 men to play one concert a week in the Plaza.[22] Federico Verea, principal musician of the band directed the first concert which included a danza, Al Despertar, by Miranda, chief musician of the band who directed the remaining concerts.[23]

A letter to the editor of The San Juan News showed that the people liked the band and urged the citizens not to miss the next concert in the Plaza Principal on Thursday night. Musical selections included a danza, Impromptu, and a cake walk, The Eagle, by Miranda.[24] At a February concert, Antonio Martínez surprised the public when he played Auld Lang Syne as a clarinet solo.[25] At the Washington birthday celebration in the Theatre, the band played the national airs, Battle Hymn, Hail Columbia, and Columbia the Gem of the Ocean.[26] For its concert on the 21st of February, it featured Puerto Rican airs, a danza, Dolores, by Miranda, selections from the opera, Bohemian Girl, and music by Tobani.[27] The band was on the dock to serenade at special occasions such as when the S.S. Rawlins took to the troops to march in the inaugural parade in Washington, D.C. (twenty men from each company and its band went), the Puerto Rican Band played La Borinqueña as they left.[28] Their April Sunday night concert included music by Mascagni, Márquez, Verdi, a hymn, Puerto Rico by Arcilagos, Bayamón by Moreno, and a danza, Sueño de amor by Morel Campos.[29]

By May 20, 1901, the Puerto Rico Provisional Regiment of Infantry consisted of eight companies of 104 enlisted men each and their officers, battalion and color sergeants and hospital stewards, a total of 866 men.[30] The members of the band included the following men: Modesto Fernández, Francisco Pasiliaria, Luis R. Miranda, Ramiro Cruzado, Mateo Cora, Manuel García, Santiago Minguez, Osvaldo Segarra, Federico Verea, José Gaudier, Gaspar Andino, Adolfo del Moral, Justo de la Paz, José Oller, Julio Ortiz, Juan Duerecut, Antonio Canido, and Silvestre Pomeras.

When the Superintendent of Schools, Dr. Brumbaugh, gave the school children 2000 flags at a Flag Day ceremony, the Regiment Band performed patriotic songs.[31] They were in the order of march in the Fourth of July parade,[32] and played La

Borinqueña and Home Sweet Home for Governor Allen as
he departed from Puerto Rico.[33] Apparently when
they performed, they had to stand, and consequently
became too tired to continue performing in this
manner. They were about to discontinue their Sunday
concert--"Their abandonment was a public
calamity,"[34] The announcement was made that the
city would provide a stand and seats for the band
enabling it to continue its concerts.[35] In
September they played a concert of works by Wagner,
Donizetti, a danza, Alma Sublime, by Morel Campos,
and two works by Miranda, American Flag Forever and
The Eagle;[36] played at a fiesta in Santurce, and a
memorial service in the Theatre.[37] From the end of
September when they played for a reception for
Governor Hunt who was visiting their post, they
remained in Cayey until November[38] when they
returned to San Juan to welcome home Colonel Buchanan
with Home Sweet Home when he returned.[39] They then
resumed weekly concerts in the Plaza.

Thanksgiving festivities included a Minstrel Show
which the band gave to entertain the U.S. military
troops on shipboard.[40] The Sunday programs in
December included the following: Sousa'a El Capitan,
Donizetti's Daughter of the Regiment, Miranda's
danzas, Alma Dichosa, Al Despertar, American Flag
Forever, danzas by Dueño Colón, Puerto Rican airs,
and selections by Verdi, Offenbach, and Albeniz.[41]
The concerts were most successful. Comment in the
newspaper on November 24: "with the concerts in the
Park, the Hotel Olimpo, and on the Plaza, there was
music galore all day yesterday. The cars were crowded
from early morn till late night and everybody seemed
to be in search of a good time."[42]

In 1902, the Puerto Rico Regiment gave weekly
concerts under the direction of Luis Miranda
(1879-1945), who was an excellent clarinetist and
also composed music for the Infantry Band. His works
included danzas, works for the piano in the style of
Gonzalo Núñez, and string quartets. In 1910, on
December 28, he was elected to the Board of Directors
of the Ateneo, and President of the Recreativa
section for 1911. He organized a prominent group, the
Club Armonico, in 1912, and later was named to the
Board of Directors of the Puerto Rico Symphony
Orchestra. Miranda entered a Quartet in D Major in a
contest in Ponce in 1913 winning third prize, $40,
and a gold medal and diploma in Class A.[43] A

substantial collection of his works are preserved in the Archivo General de Puerto Rico.

At his band concerts in addition to one of his own works, Miranda included music by Tobani, Mills, Farrar, Molloy, Panella, Fabian, Witt, as well as Sousa's The Liberty Bell, selections from the opera, Faust, by Gounod, Don Juanito by Suppé, a polka, Masquerade, by Laurendau, a cakewalk, Hula, Hula, by Alstyne, march, Under the Double Eagle, by J.F. Wagner, and previously mentioned works by Morel Campos.[44] There was a performance at the Spanish Club under the direction of Sgt. Pomares of Lares,[45] a Washington's birthday concert for children in the San Juan Theatre,[46] and most of the previously mentioned titles were repeated at each of the concerts,[47] until finally, at the end of April, an editorial remarked that the people who heard the Regiment Band on Sunday had mentioned the antiquity of the numbers played. The fault lay with the officials who had not ordered new music. The band still practiced every day but had only musty music to perform and received no compensation for performing in public. The editor felt that as soon as it would receive new music it would show a decided improvement.[48] After that it participated in a Corpus Christi feast day procession in June, playing march music under the direction of Miranda,[49] performed with the Police and Charity School Bands for the Fourth of July parade,[50] but then left for Cayey, leaving only one band in San Juan. That ended the Sunday concerts for the time being.[51]

In September it was announced that the Regiment Band had returned from Cayey and would resume its concerts in the Plaza, the first in several months.[52] Programs included music by Sousa, Strauss, Jones, Mills, and Miranda, under whose direction it performed.[53] There was a large attendance at the October concert and the new selection, Description of Indian Life, was loudly applauded.[54] November programs were also well attended, and the band received many encores. Miranda had just composed a beautiful romanza to a text by Perez Losada, and his works Puerto Rico, a march, La Perla, Alma Dichosa, and Idealidad were performed as well as works by Gounod, Volestad, Kretschner, de Witt, and Losey. They gave concerts each week in November, playing in Borínquen Park on November 17 and at the Arsenal on the 26th.[55] In December it played in a parade with the Charity School Band to escort Admiral Dewey, when he arrived on the S.S. Mayflower, from the ship to the Palace.[56] The year ended with the band playing during a reception at the Palace when Governor Hunt's daughter, Elizabeth, was presented to society. The Police Band played for the arriving guests in the courtyard, and the Regiment Band played in the garden, which was ablaze with Japanese lanterns.[57]

During 1903 the Regiment Band joined forces with the Police Band and the Charity School Band at several functions. In March the three bands played in the Plaza for about 5000 people to enjoy music and fireworks and "they never played better."[58] The Regiment Band itself played for a variety of occasions during the year--at the Naval Station, while the band from the Ship Massachusetts went to the graveyard during a service for the sailors who died when an 8 inch gun exploded aboard the ship.[59] They played for Barracks dances, and every Monday, Wednesday, and Friday, after the battalion drill, they marched in a dress parade and gave a concert in the Plaza de Armas.[60] They marched in a dress parade in honor of Alice Roosevelt on her island tour,[61] and with the Police Band furnished music for the Governor's reception at the Río Piedras gardens in honor of Alice Roosevelt.[62] In April they played on the deck of the Ship Algonquin before it left for Pensacola, Florida and also at a reception at Santa Catalina with the Police Band.[63] During all of their concerts, Miranda's music was performed.[64]

On July 4th, with the Police Band, the Regiment Band rendered a number of beautiful selections, "the strains of which completely filled the large auditorium" of the theatre.[65] The same review stated that the drill by the Puerto Rico Regiment was particularly good, as was the clarinet solo by Francisco Verar, leader of the Insular Police Band. On July 30th the Regiment Band played appropriate selections at the Misa Pontifical de Requiem in the Cathedral in memory of Pope Leo XIII who had died.[66] They had just returned from Saint Louis where they had performed during Puerto Rico Day at the World's Fair.[67] In September they played an overture "in masterly style" for a program at the Ateneo,[68] and in November played for a funeral for the mother of two of their band members--Antonio and

Francisco Vargas' mother, Carmen Vargas.[69] In November they attracted a great deal of attention with the playing of _Ave Maria_ and other selections.[70]

The Puerto Rico Regiment Band continued to perform weekly concerts in the Plaza during 1903 but were not listed in the newspapers in 1904 until they resumed their concerts in the Plaza on Sundays in May.[71] It continued to be listed in the newspapers until the end of October. In December, Miranda received high praise for his new march, _President Roosevelt_, which he had dedicated to the President,[72] and which was performed by his band in Baldorioty Plaza.[73]

The Regiment Band under Miranda's direction in 1905, played for a dance in January at San Cristobal Castle and was not in the news again until March when it gave a concert in Plaza Baldorioty, playing music by Burton, C. Gómez, Gounod, Wagner, Keiser, Sousa, Miranda, and ending with the national hymn.[74] Miranda presented several new titles of danzas he had composed during the summer months and throughout the fall. In November he was credited with a "brilliant concert,"[75] they celebrated the holy day December 8th by parading in the streets early in the morning playing Spanish airs,[76] and ended the year with two more new compositions, _La Diana_ and _Aires Puertorriqueños_.

6. THE BOYS'CHARITY SCHOOL BAND

As early as 1875, a music class under the direction of Rosario Aruti was established at the Asilo de Beneficencia (Charity School). In 1883, Sandalio Callejo succeeded Aruti, after which Jaime Bastard was the director. He was replaced by Francisco Verar until 1898.[1] Very often during the holiday season, bands of children would appear in the streets to serenade the tourists. One such band of children walked the streets of Mayagüez singing songs to the accompaniment of guitars, piccolos, flutes, tambourines, and a triangle. (The tambourine was also quickly converted to a tray in order to solicit donations.)[2] No leader is mentioned nor was there a name given to the band. The Charity School Band does not appear in the news until the end of 1900 when it performed several patriotic airs.[3] It does not appear again until 1901, and seemed to have grown progressively more active throughout the decade under the new leadership of Juan Viñolo Sanz. The boys' band played when the Board of Charities gave a party for the Girls' and Boys' Charity Schools of Santurce. There were about 200 children and fifteen Sisters of Charity.[4] The band was augmented in March by ten or twelve new members, and an order was placed for enough new instruments to fully equip the organization.[5] It performed with other bands when Governor Herbert Allen arrived on the island, the children paraded, and there was a concert in the Plaza with fireworks and a speech by the President of the Ateneo.[6]

About 2000 children marched in the Fourth of July parade in 1901 and the Boys' Charity School Band furnished music with other bands. The boys next appeared in the news when it gave a concert in October during a lawn party at the Olimpo.[7]

In 1902 they played at a Washington's birthday celebration in Arecibo, alternating with the Puerto Rico Regiment Band.[8] They were listed as the Banda Beneficencia or as La Banda de la Niños de Asilo de Santurce and played for Flag Day when the children paraded from Plaza Colón to Plaza Principal, where there were recitations, speeches, and a flag drill.[9] In July, the band played in the Plaza on Sunday under the direction of its leader Juan Viñolo. The program included a medley of marches by Sousa, Home Sweet Home, a polka, Canario by Viñolo, La Culebra by Morel Campos, and the Star Spangled Banner.[10] Their next concert featured works by Viñolo, Armand, Teneira, and Margarita by Tavárez.[11] They gave a farewell concert in August, a Sunday concert in the Plaza Principal,[12] but played occasional programs during the fall of the year. In September they performed in Borínquen Park in Santurce for a fiesta in honor of San Mateo,[13] in October they participated with other bands in a Plaza concert in honor of Governor Hunt,[14] and played in December in the gardens of the Hotel Olimpo.[15]

In March of 1903 they performed with the Police Band and Regiment Band for about 5000 people in the Plaza,[16] and were invited to perform for Bishop Blenk on his third anniversary on July 2, [17] and were in the Fourth of July parade.[18] The children apparently performed exceedingly well. An editorial in The San Juan News regarding their capabilities stated that they were being sent to the Saint Louis Exposition. "A most remarkable result has certainly been attained with these boys and the musical director whose painstaking skill has brought it about is deserving of all the praise for the results he has accomplished."[19] The children ranged from 10 to 14 years of age. At the Fair in Saint Louis, they played "with the same magnificent impression."[20] In September in spite of the city officials dislike of Governor Hunt, three bands performed for the Governor's return. The Boys' Charity School Band paraded along with the others.[21]

The Charity School Band appeared to schedule only four concerts in 1904. In February it offered in Plaza Baldorioty, playing Director of Charities by Viñolo, and works by Tavárez, Ingraham, Andril, and Nieto.[22] In May it performed with the Police Band at a charity benefit, playing a romanza, La Patria by Viñolo and Whistling Rufus by Blake.[23] On July 14, under the direction of Cecilia Klein, public school teacher, a fiesta was organized at the Charity School. The children's band performed for the program which was given for Governor Beekman Winthrop.[24] In December there was a fiesta which featured the children's band at Christmas time.[25]

The children were fairly active in 1905. For the month of June their program featured works by their director Viñolo, Bellini, Tavárez, Armand, and Clausens.[26] In July it played El Director by Vinolo, Serenata by Schubert, a danza, La Melancolía, by Tavárez, and other selections.[27] For the feast of Saint Matthew in September, the band gave a program in the gardens of the school, playing the following program: Fantasía de bombardino (euphonium); mazurka, Cristinita; danza, La Reina de Carnaval; Polaka de concierto obligado a clarinete by Viñolo; Estrella Confidente by V. Robaida, and the Star Spangled Banner.[28] The band performed during a program with the Regiment and Police Bands in September in honor of Baldorioty de Castro at the Ateneo Puertorriqueño, playing a romanza, Patria by Viñolo, which won a prize in the Ateneo contest, and closing the program with Estrella Confidente.[29] In October it performed again, playing arrangements by Viñolo, Miserere from Verdi's Il Trovatore, Intermezzo from Cavalleria Rusticana by Mascagni, The

Holy City, a polka with clarinet obligato by Viñolo, and one of his two-steps, El Teniente Iturrondo, closing with both La Borinqueña and the Star Spangled Banner.[30] When Bishop Blenk and other prominent citizens attended ceremonies at the Charity School in Santurce, the band played hymns and received great applause.[31] They gave concerts in the gardens of the school on November 11th and 17th, performing a combination of works by Viñolo, selections from operas and lesser known works.[32]

The Charity School Band opened 1906 with a concert in honor of Arthur E. Estabrook of Boston, Massachusetts, at the end of January. The program included the following works: Marcha Triunfal de la Bandera by Viñolo, The Holy City, Intermezzo from Cavalleria Rusticana, selections from Lucia di Lammermoor, Spanish Love Song by Gonzalo Núñez, waltz, Veloz with cornet obligato by Viñolo, and danza, La Reina del Carnaval, by Viñolo.[33] Concerts were given on Saturdays in the gardens of the school from June through August and featured works by Viñolo and included a variety of other composer's works.

7. JUVENTUD DEL COMERCIO BAND

In January, 1901, the owner of the Fashion Bazaar invited everyone to attend a concert by Manuel Tizol's new city band on a Saturday evening.[1] This band does not appear in the news again. In 1903, he organized a band named Juventud del Comercio. It offered weekly concerts in the public square and according to Callejo, because this ensemble's existence depended upon voluntary subscriptions, the band ended soon.[2] The newspapers show that the Juventud del Comercio was active after its formation through April, 1905. Tizol composed as well as directed the band and five of his works are preserved in the Archivo General de Puerto Rico (Numbers 1915-1919).

The Comercio Band performed in the Plaza Principal from July through December of 1903. Its programs usually included works by Tizol, Duchesne, Dueño Colón, pieces by Spanish composers, and the usual selections from standard operas. It was first in the news when it performed at Toa Alta in April, and next was greatly applauded in June.[3] It gave a

106

total of fourteen concerts, from July 17, 1903, to December 18th, 1903.[4] It was the custom of bands to serenade business houses on New Years Day and also to awaken the people for Mass on a holiday. During the Christmas season, the Comercio Band played each morning at 4 or 5 a.m. and the people were awakened by their "noise."[5] Programs included works by Puerto Rican composers and other well-known band composers as well as transcriptions of movements of Beethoven symphonies.

Tizol's Juventud del Comercio Band performed quite regularly during 1904. In January concerts included works by Tizol, Verdi, Chueca, Chapi, and Ríos Ovalle.[6] The week of the 29th, Tizol's band gave the fourth concert in Baldorioty Park that week.[7] In February its program in the Plaza included works by Rossini, Verdi, Espinosa, Milpager, and Márquez.[8] It also played selections at the marina on Sunday evening, February 21.[9] In March at the Plaza Baldorioty the band played a danza, Teresa by Dueño Colón, Viva España by Escobes, and works by Montes, Wagner, Martin, and Marquis.[10] On March 18 in the Plaza Principal it included El Manolillo by Duchesne, and works by Marquis, Montes, Waldteufel, Drigo, and Caballero.[11] The program at the marina March 24 included a two-step, El Canario by Viñolo, a danza, Idilio by Morel Campos, Sinfonía in F Major by Dueño Colón, and works by Caballero, Mascagni, and Valverde.[12] At the end of March, the band accompanied a zarzuela in the Theatre.[13] In April its repertoire included Vibraciones del Alma by Ríos Ovalle, El Buen Humor and La Perlita by Duchesne, and works by Giménez, Verdi, Suppé, Chapi, Márquez, Erviti, and Milpager.[14]

The Juventud del Comercio Band gave weekly concerts in June, playing several arrangements by Tizol and repeating a waltz, Los Fantoches, with variations for two euphoniums by Dueño Colón.[15] In July its programs featured Viva España by Fernando Callejo, and works by Ríos Ovalle, Ecos de mi Patria by Duchesne, and music by Tizol.[16] Tizol's weekly concerts in Plaza Baldorioty in August added tangos by himself, and No comas fósforo by Morel Campos to the repertoire.[17] In September the band played in both Plaza Baldorioty and Plaza de Armas and for the fiesta of the Patron Saint in the church in Santurce, a total of eight concerts. Tizol's arrangements were played, works by Marquis, Giménez, Waldteufel,

Escobes, Rossini, Ríos Ovalle, and the danza. Teresa, by Dueño Colón.[18] At Plaza Baldorioty in October the band played Margarita by Tavárez and other works.[19] In November it performed in Río Piedras, including works by Duchesne, Morel Campos, and others mentioned above.[20] It also performed on New Years Eve in Río Piedras to complete the activities of the year.[21]

Tizol's band was heard in March, April, and November of 1905, and were always greeted with enthusiasm. Their programs included works by Escobes, Bellini, Cruz, Márquez, Waldteufel, Verdi, Gilbert and Sullivan, Meyerbeer, Donizetti, and Giménez.[22]

Tizol had other ensembles that performed throughout the next years, instrumental ensembles that entertained with Tizol conducting or playing bass. His Sextet featured Julián Andino on concert violin, Manuel Castelón on violin 2, Sergio Lecompte playing viola, Franz Rooms, cello, Tizol, contra bass, J. Monclova, flute, and Justo Pastor Torres, piano.[23] The next year he formed an Octet, adding Julián Lecompte, violin 1, Domingo Andino, violin 2, Rafael Márquez, flute, Andrés Fernández, oboe, Joaquín Burset, piano.[24] Later that year, Tizol formed another Juventud del Comercio[25] and was recorded by Columbia Records.[26] Most of the programs by all of the bands are similar as the bands reach a certain level of performance--selections from operas, movements from symphonies, marches, and many many danzas by Puerto Rican composers which always appeared to be favorites. In the following section, the Puerto Rican composers whose music was so popular during this era will be considered.

1. Ateneo Puertorriqueño

1. Ateneo Puertorriqueño. San Juan: Talleres Gráficos Interamericanos, Inc., 1966, n.p.

2. SJN, VIII/74 (March 31, 1903), 4, and BM, LXV/75 (March 31, 1903), 1.

3. SJN, VIII/205 (September 9, 1903), 5.

4. His presidency was announced in SJN, VIII/179 (August 8, 1903), 4.

5. Ibid., VIII/205 (September 9, 1903), 5.

6. Ibid., VIII/217 (September 23, 1903), 1.

7. Callejo, p. 148.

8. Certámenes del Ateneo Puetorriqueño, 1877–1970.

9. BM, LXIX/116 (May 17, 1907), 2.

10. Ibid., LXX/184 (August 5, 1908), 1.

11. Ateneo Puertorriqueño (1960), n.p.

12. BM, LXX/188 (August 10, 1908), 1, and LXX/189 (August 11, 1908), 3.

13. Callejo, p. 185.

14. Certamenes . . . , n.p.

15. CM 73-4: La significación de la obra de José Quintón, Homenaje y develación de su retrato al óleo. Participants: Luis Antonio Ramírez, Amaury Veray, and Carlos Gadea-Pico.

16. CM 71-32: Don Braulio Dueño Colón: músico y compositor. Homenaje y develación de su retrato al óleo. Participants: Luis Antonio Ramírez, Isabel Gutiérrez del Arroyo, Jesús María Sanromá, Emilio S. Belaval (Tenor). Chorus from La Escuela B. Dueño Colón, and the Church of the Lutherans in Bayamón.

17. CM 68-31: Don Jesús Figueroa Iriarte, Homenaje. Palabras de Don Antonio Corretjer.

18. SJN, VIII/206 (September 10, 1903), 2.

***

2. The Music in the Churches Notes

1. E.g., Gutiérrez and Ledesma mentioned above, and see Arturo V. Dávila, "José Campeche, maestro de música," Revista del Instituto de Cultura Puertorriqueña, III/8 (July-September, 1960), 14-16. He taught plainsong and organ to the Carmelite nuns at El Convento, Old San Juan (now a government-owned hotel). Also see Dávila's "El platero Domingo De Andino, 1737-1829), maestro de música de Campeche," Revista del Instituto de Cultura Puertorriqueña, V/6 (July-September, 1962), 36-38.

2. On the front of the hospital is a bronze plaque noting that Fray Junipero Serra, O.F.M., had stopped there on his way to California from October 18 to November 2, 1749.

***

3. The Celebration of Holy Days Notes

1. María Teresa Babín. La cultura de Puerto Rico. San Juan, P.R.: Instituto de Cultura Puertorriqueña, 1970, p. 93.

2. Josefina Gil de Prann. Typical Christmas Customs in Puerto Rico. San Juan: Imp. Correo Dominical, 1929, pp. 16-24.

3. SJN, VIII/8 (January 11, 1903), 3.

4. Ibid., VIII/205 (September 9, 1903), 1.

5. Ibid., III/103 (August 23, 1899), 1.

6. BM, LXIII/143 (June 22, 1901), 2.

7. Ibid., LXVIII/132 (June 6, 1906), 5.

8. Ibid., LXVIII/143 (June 19, 1906), 5.

9. Ibid., LXVIII/150 (June 27, 1906), 5.

***

4. The Band Concerts in the City Parks
Early Bands and Insular Police Band Notes

1. Some of the Puerto Rican newspapers were not available for certain dates either in Puerto Rico or in the Library of Congress. Some had deteriorated; some were illegible. As the years progressed from 1898 there were advertisements for band concerts but no director name or program given. Some advertisements for band concerts did not specify which band was to perform. The Charity Band of children usually concluded with the Puerto Rican hymn. By 1906 the Insular Police Band played both the Star Spangled Banner and La Borinqueña at the close of the concert.

2. BM, LXIII/283 (December 9, 1901), 2.

3. SJN, IV/61 (February 17, 1900), 1.

4. BM, LXI/7 (January 7, 1899), 1.

5. Ibid., LXI/11 (January 12, 1899), 2. It played American hymns including the Star Spangled Banner, Hail Columbia, and La Borinqueña.

6. El País, V/150 (January 27, 1899), 3.

7. BM, LXI/92 (April 19, 1899), 1; El País, V/198 (August 24, 1899), 1; SJN, III/113 (September 3, 1899), 5, which mentioned it stopped by September because the city was paying 236 pesos a month for its services and had to withdraw the funds.

8. SJN, V/52 (August 31, 1900), 1.

9. Ibid., VI/128 (June 3, 1901), 8.

10. Ibid., VI/232 (October 5, 1901), 5; VI/245 (October 20, 1901), 6.

11. Ibid., VI/296 (December 21, 1901), 4.

12. Ibid., V/143 (December 19, 1900), 1.

13. Ibid., IV/7 (January 6, 1900), 1; IV/33 (January 21, 1900), 1; IV/47 (January 30, 1900), 1; IV/79 (February 18, 1900), 1.

14. Ibid., IV/81 (February 20, 1900), 1.

15. Ibid., IV/267 (June 17, 1900), 1.

16. Ibid., IV/97 (March 4, 1900), 5.

17. Ibid., IV/178 (April 24, 1900), 1.

18. Ibid., V/58 (September 8, 1900), 1.

19. Ibid., V/91 (October 18, 1900), 1.

20. Ibid., IV/293 (July 4, 1900), 1, 5.

21. Ibid., IV/308 (July 14, 1900), 1; IV/316 (July 19, 1900), 1;
    IV/320 (July 21, 1900), 2.

22. Ibid., V/128 (December 1, 1900), 4.

23. Ibid., V/34 (August 10, 1900), 1.

24. Ibid., V/128 (December 1, 1900), 1.

25. United States House of Representatives 56th Congress, 2nd
    Session, Document No. 137, p. 77.

26. El País, V/198 (August 24, 1899), 1.

27. SJN, IV/51 (February 1, 1900), 1.

28. Ibid., IV/55 (February 3, 1900), 1; IV/87 (February 24,
    1900), 1.

29. Ibid., IV/91 (February 27, 1900), 1.

30. Ibid., IV/286 (June 29, 1900), 1.

31. Ibid., IV/293 (July 4, 1900), 1.

32. Ibid., VI/52 (March 3, 1901), 1.

33. Ibid., VI/59 (March 12, 1901), 8.

34. BM, LXIII/126 (June 1, 1901), 1, and SJN, VI/134 (June 9,
    1901), 1.

35. SJN, VI/146 (June 25, 1901), 8.

36. El País, VII/159 (July 5, 1901), 1.

37. SJN, VI/161 (July 14, 1901), 1.

38. Register of Puerto Rico for 1903. San Juan: Louis Z. Tuzo &
    Co., 1903, p. 140.

112

39. SJN, VI/205 (September 5, 1901), 8.

40. Ibid., VI/209 (September 11, 1901), 8.

41. Ibid., VI/210 (September 12, 1901), 3.

42. Ibid., VI/212 (September 14, 1901), 8.

43. La Democracia, XI/2992 (September 17, 1901), 1.

44. United States House of Representatives Document No. 5557, 60th Congress, 2nd Session, Document No. 1204, Annual Report of the Auditor of Puerto Rico, George Cabot Ward, and Document No. 5393, Annual Report of the Governor, 1908, p. 102.

45. SJN, VI/223 (September 25, 1901), 5; VI/230 (October 3, 1901), 1.

46. Ibid., VI/233 (October 6, 1901), 1, and El País, VII/233 (October 12, 1901).

47. Ibid., V/239 (October 13, 1901), 4.

48. Ibid., VI/264 (November 12, 1901), 2; VI/268 (November 17, 1901), 3.

49. Ibid., VI/300 (December 27, 1900), 8.

50. Ibid., VII/55 (March 6, 1902), 5; El País, VIII/51 (March 3, 1902), 1.

51. SJN, VIII/63 (March 18, 1902), 8; BM, LXIV/64 (March 18, 1902), 1.

52. El País, VIII/107 (May 13, 1902), 1.

53. BM, LXIV/196 (December 23, 1902), 7; SJN, VII/384 (December 24, 1902), 7.

54. SJN, VII/313 (October 1, 1902), 3; VII/319 (October 8, 1902), 5; VII/326 (October 15, 1902), 4; VII/331 (October 22, 1902), 2; VII/337 (October 29, 1902), 5.

55. Ibid., VII/88 (April 17, 1902), 8.

56. Ibid., VII/212 (May 27, 1902), 1.

57. Ibid., VII/214 (May 29, 1902), 8.

58. Ibid., VII/244 (July 4, 1902), 7.

59. Ibid., VII/248 (July 10, 1902), 5.

60. Ibid., VII/261 (July 25, 1902), 8.

61. Ibid., VII/286 (August 28, 1902), 8.

62. Ibid., VII/296 (September 11, 1902), 8.

63. BM, LXIV/224 (September 28, 1902), 2.

64. SJN, VII/323 (October 12, 1902), 1; VII/330 (October 21, 1902), 1902, 8.

65. BM, LXIV/267 (November 18, 1902), 3; SJN, VII/355 (November 19, 1902), 1.

66. BM, LXIV/280 (December 3, 1902), 1.

67. Ibid., LXIV/282 (December 5, 1902), 7.

68. SJN, VII/374 (December 12, 1902), 3.

69. Ibid., VII/389 (December 31, 1902), 3.

70. Ibid., VIII/6 (January 8, 1903), 8.

71. Register of Puerto Rico for 1903, p. 143.

72. SJN, VIII/212 (September 17, 1903), 1.

73. Ibid., VIII/167 (July 24, 1903), 2; VIII/217 (September 23, 1903), 2.

74. Ibid., VIII/137 (June 16, 1903), 5.

75. Ibid., IX/25 (January 30, 1904), 8.

76. Ibid., IX/28 (February 3, 1904), 6; IX/35 (February 9, 1904), 7; IX/36 (February 10, 1904), 8; IX/40 (February 17, 1904), 3; IX/67 (March 22, 1904), 1.

77. Ibid., IX/68 (March 24, 1904), 1.

78. Ibid., IX/73 (March 30, 1904), 3.

79. Ibid., IX/77 (April 6, 1904), 4; IX/84 (April 13, 1904), 4; IX/90 (April 20, 1904), 1; IX/96 (April 27, 1904), 3.

114

80. Ibid., IX/103 (May 5, 1904), 5.

81. Ibid., IX/114 (May 18, 1904), 5; IX/120 (May 25, 1904), 1.

82. Ibid., IX/138 (June 16, 1904), 4.

83. Ibid., IX/146 (June 24, 1904), 3.

84. Ibid., IX/147 (June 25, 1904), 8.

85. Ibid., IX/150 (June 30, 1904), 4.

86. Ibid., IX/154 (July 6, 1904), 1.

87. BM, LXVI/155 (July 6, 1904), 2; LXVI/160 (July 12, 1904), 2; LXVI/167 (July 20, 1904), 2.

88. SJN, IX/194 (August 23, 1904), 1.

89. Ibid., IX/207 (August 7, 1904), 3; BM, LXVI/183 (August 9, 1904), 2; LXVI/189 (August 16, 1904), 2.

90. SJN, IX/195 (August 24, 1904), 4; Ibid., IX/220 (August 31, 1904), 4; BM, LXVI/201 (August 30, 1904), 2.

91. BM, LXVI/206 (September 6, 1904), 2; LXVI/212 (September 13, 1904), 2, 7; LXVI/224 (September 27, 1904), 1.

92. SJN, IX/273 (November 22, 1904), 1; BM, LXVI/271 (November 22, 1904), 2.

93. SJN, IX/298 (December 21, 1904), 1; IX/304 (December 28, 1904), 5.

94. BM, LXVII/151 (July 5, 1905), 2.

95. Ibid., LXVII/164 (July 20, 1905), 2.

96. Ibid., LXVII/221 (September 27, 1905), 7.

97. Ibid., LXVII/264 (November 16, 1905), 4.

98. Ibid., LXVII/285 (December 12, 1905), 4.

99. Ibid., LXVII/294 (December 22, 1905), 4.

100. Ibid., LXVII/300 (December 30, 1905), 4.

101. Ibid., LXVII/77 (April 4, 1905), 2.

102. Ibid., LXVII/145 (June 27, 1905), 2.

103. Ibid., LXVII/149 (July 1, 1905), 2.

104. Ibid., LXVII/151 (July 5, 1905), 7.

105. Ibid.

106. Ibid., LXVII/157 (July 12, 1905), 4.

107. Ibid., LXVII/171 (July 29, 1905), 2.

108. Ibid., LXVII/191 (August 22, 1905), 4.

109. Ibid., LXVII/197 (August 29, 1905), 4.

110. Ibid.

111. Ibid., LXVII/201 (September 2, 1905), 4.

112. Ibid., LXVII/203 (September 5, 1905), 4.

113. Ibid., LXVII/224 (September 30, 1905), 4.

114. Ibid., LXVII/230 (October 7, 1905), 5.

115. Ibid., LXVII/236 (October 14, 1905), 4.

116. Ibid., LXVII/237 (October 16, 1905), 7.

117. Ibid., LXVII/242 (October 21, 1905), 4.

118. Ibid.

119. Ibid., LXVII/283 (December 9, 1905), 4.

120. Ibid., LXVII/295 (December 23, 1905), 7.

121. Ibid.

122. Ibid., LXVII/60 (March 13, 1906), 1.

123. Ibid., LXVII/143 (June 19, 1906), 4.

124. Ibid., LXVIII/160 (July 10, 1906), 2.

***

5. The Puerto Rico Regiment Band Notes

1. United States 59th Congress, 1st Session, No. 4910, Document No. 8, Fifth Annual Report of the Governor of Puerto Rico, Beekman Winthrop, December, 1905, p. 33.

2. United States Vol.: Puerto Rico; Regiment Orders, Letters Sent MTD Battle/Infantry/A.G.O. War With Spain [in the National Archives, Washington, D.C.] Orders #16, pp. 51-53.

3. Ibid., Orders #28 and 22, pp. 53-54, n.d.

4. Ibid., pp. 54-56.

5. Ibid., Orders #32, p. 63.

6. Ibid., Orders #26, pp. 15, 17.

7. SJN, IV/186 (April 28, 1900), 3.

8. Ibid., IV/191 (May 2, 1900), 3.

9. Ibid., IV/237 (May 30, 1900), 1.

10. United States Vols., p. 79.

11. SJN, IV/225 (May 23, 1900), 1, and IV/253 (June 9, 1900), 1.

12. Ibid., V/52 (August 31, 1900), 1.

13. BM, LXII/184 (August 15, 1900), 2.

14. United States Vols., Orders #40, p. 3, n.d.

15. Ibid., G Orders, #40, p. 17.

16. Ibid., G. Orders, #41, p. 18.

17. SJN, V/95 (October 23, 1900), 1.

18. Ibid., V/134 (December 8, 1900), 1.

19. Ibid., V/136 (December 11, 1900), 1.

20. Ibid., V/140 (December 15, 1900), 4.

21. BM, LXII/296 (December 27, 1900), 2, and SJN, V/151 (December 29, 1900), 1.

22. SJN, VI/6 (January 8, 1901), 1.

23. Ibid., VI/9 (January 11, 1901), 4.

24. Ibid., VI/14 (January 17, 1901), 1, and VI/26 (January 31, 1901), 3.

25. Ibid., VI/28 (February 2, 1901), 3.

26. Ibid., VI/42 (February 19, 1901), 6, and VI/46 (February 24, 1901), 5.

27. Ibid., VI/45 (February 22, 1901), 1.

28. Ibid., VI/44 (February 21, 1901), 1, and VI/47 (February 26, 1901), 1.

29. Ibid., VI/96 (April 28, 1901), 7.

30. Regiment Orders/Special Orders Puerto Rico Provisional Infantry Regiment, June, 1901 to December, 1901. National Archives [Washington, D.C.] Navy and Old Army Division, [R.G. 395: Entry 5863].

31. SJN, VI/239 (June 15, 1901), 1.

32. Ibid., VI/154 (July 5, 1901), 8.

33. SJN, VI/101 (July 14, 1901), 1.

34. Ibid., VI/168 (July 23, 1901), 1.

35. Ibid., VI/171 (July 27, 1901), 4, and VI/173 (July 30, 1901), 3.

36. Ibid., VI/207 (September 8, 1901), 5.

37. Ibid., VI/211 (September 13, 1901), 1, and VI/216 (September 19, 1901), 1.

38. Ibid., VI/227 (September 29, 1901), 1, and VI/262 (November 9, 1901), 8.

39. Ibid., VI/266 (November 15, 1901), 1.

40. Ibid., VI/278 (November 30. 1901), 3.

41. Ibid., VI/279 (December 1, 1901), 3; VI/297 (December 27, 1901), 5, and VI/320 (December 30, 1901), 8.

42. BM, LXVIII./272 (November 25, 1901), 2.

43. United States Vol., Orders #40, p. 3, n.d.

44. SJN, VII/10 (January 12, 1902), 7; VII/16 (January 19, 1902), 3; VII/22 (January 26, 1902), 8; VII/28 (February 4, 1902), 8; VII/34 (February 9, 1902), 8, and VII/41 (February 16, 1901), 5.

45. SJN, VII/17 (January 21, 1902), 6.

46. Ibid., VII/45 (February 21, 1902), 5.

47. BM, LXIV/50 (March 1, 1902), 3; LXIV/84 (April 12, 1902), 3; LXIV/103 (May 3, 1902), 2, and SJN, VII/68 (March 13, 1902), 4.

48. SJN, VII/92 (April 22, 1902), 8.

49. Ibid., VII/217 (June 3, 1902), 8.

50. Ibid., VII/244 (July 4, 1902), 7.

51. Ibid., VII/248 (July 10, 1902), 5.

52. BM, LXIV/206 (September 6, 1902), 2.

53. SJN, VII/311 (September 28, 1902), 8.

54. Ibid., VII/318 (October 7, 1902), 8.

55. BM, LXIV/260 (November 10, 1902), 3; LXIV/153 (November 1, 1902), 7; LXIV/166 (November 17, 1902), 2; LXIV/274 (November 26, 1902), 3; SJN, VII/353 (November 16, 1902), 5, and VII/359 (November 23, 1902), 7.

56. SJN, VII/384 (December 24, 1902), 1.

57. Ibid., 1, 5.

58. Ibid., VII/69 (March 25, 1903), 3; VIII/77 (April 3, 1903), 1.

59. Ibid., VIII/14 (January 18, 1903), 1.

60. Ibid., VIII/28 (February 5, 1903), 8; BM, LXV/27 (February 2, 1903), 3, and LXV/39 (February 16, 1903), 3.

61. SJN, VIII/67 (March 21, 1903), 5.

62. Ibid., VIII/68 (March 22, 1903), 1.

63. Ibid., VIII/80 (April 8, 1903), 8; BM, LXV/78 (April 3, 1903), 3.

64. SJN, VIII/89 (April 19, 1903), 6; VIII/95 (April 26, 1903), 4; VIII/101 (May 3, 1903), 5; VIII/136 (June 14, 1903), 1; VIII/141 (June 21, 1903), 5; VIII/147 (June 28, 1903), 2.

65. Ibid., VIII/152 (July 4, 1903), 8.

66. Ibid., VIII/164 (July 21, 1903), 1; VIII/171 (July 30, 1903), 5 and 8.

67. Ibid., VIII/216 (September 22, 1903), 3.

68. Ibid. VIII/217 (September 23, 1903), 1.

69. Ibid., VIII/261 (November 12, 1903), 1.

70. Ibid., 4. No titles given.

71. Puerto Rico Journal, I/1 (May 16, 1904), 2.

72. SJN, IX/290 (December 11, 1904), 3.

73. Ibid., IX/291 (December 13, 1904), 1.

74. BM, LXVII/16 (January 20, 1905), 2; LXVII/69 (March 25, 1905), 1.

75. Ibid., LXVII/244 (October 24, 1905), 4; LXVII/273 (November 27, 1905), 1.

76. Ibid., LXVII/282 (December 7, 1905), 4.

***

6. The Boys' Charity School Band Notes

1. Héctor Campos Parsi, Música. La Gran Enciclopedia de Puerto Rico, VII (San Juan [Madrid: C. Corredera] 1976), p. 224.

2. SJN, IV/49 (January 31, 1900), 2.

3. Ibid., V/144 (December 20, 1900), 1.

4. Ibid., VI/6 (January 8, 1901), 1.

5. BM, LXIII/74 (March 29, 1901), 3.

6. _SJN_, VI/119 (May 22, 1901), 1, and VI/120 (May 23, 1901), 1.

7. _Ibid._, VI/228 (October 1, 1901), 8.

8. _Ibid._, VII/45 (February 21, 1902), 3.

9. _Ibid._, VII/226 (June 13, 1902), 5.

10. _Ibid._, VII/250 (July 12, 1902), 4.

11. _Ibid._, VII/256 (July 19, 1902), 3.

12. _Ibid._, VII/268 (August 3, 1902), 7.

13. _Ibid._, VII/301 (September 17, 1902), 4, and VII/304 (September 20, 1902), 8.

14. _The Puerto Rico Times_, I/1 (October 17, 1902), 2.

15. _BM_, LXIV/299 (December 27, 1902), 3.

16. _SJN_, VIII/69 (March 25, 1903), 3.

17. _Ibid._, VIII/149 (July 1, 1903), 1.

18. _Ibid._, VIII/151 (July 3, 1903), 7.

19. _Ibid._, VIII/174 (August 2, 1903), 2.

20. _Ibid._, VIII/216 (September 22, 1903), 3.

21. _Ibid._, VIII/223 (September 30, 1903), 1.

22. _Ibid._, IX/28 (February 3, 1904), 3.

23. _Ibid._, IX/103 (May 5, 1904), 5.

24. _BM_, LXVI/162 (July 14, 1904), 2.

25. _Ibid._, LXVI/295 (December 23, 1904), 2.

26. _Ibid._, LXVII/130 (June 3, 1905), 3, and LXVII/138 (June 17, 1905), 1.

27. _Ibid._, LXVII/152 (July 6, 1905), 3.

28. _Ibid._, LXVII/216 (September 21, 1905), 1.

29. _Ibid._, LXVII/224 (September 30, 1905), 4.

30. Ibid., LXVII/249 (October 30, 1905), 7.

31. Ibid., LXVII/251 (November 1, 1905), 2.

32. Ibid., LXVII/260 (November 11, 1905), 7, and LXVII/265 (November 17, 1905), 2.

33. Ibid., LXVIII/24 (January 29, 1906), 4.

***

7. The Juventud del Comercio Band Notes

1. SJN, VI/15 (January 18, 1901), 4.

2. Callejo, p. 70.

3. BM, LXV/196 (April 27, 1903), 5, and LXV/143 (June 20, 1903), 2.

4. SJN, VIII/300 (December 31, 1903), 8.

5. Ibid., VIII/297 (December 25, 1903), 4.

6. Ibid., IX/6 (January 8, 1904), 5; IX/12 (January 15, 1904), 7, and IX/20 (January 24, 1904), 4.

7. Ibid., IX/24 (January 29, 1904), 1.

8. Ibid., IX/30 (February 5, 1904), 7.

9. Ibid., IX/44 (February 21, 1904), 4.

10. Ibid., IX/59 (March 11, 1904), 6.

11. Ibid., IX/64 (March 18, 1904), 3.

12. Ibid., IX/68 (March 24, 1904), 7.

13. Ibid., IX/70 (March 26, 1904), 4.

14. Ibid., IX/79 (April 8, 1904), and IX/92 (April 22, 1904), 4.

15. Ibid., IX/127 (June 3, 1904), 4; IX/133 (June 10, 1904), 5, and IX/139 (June 17, 1904), 4.

16. BM, LXVI/156 (July 7, 1904), 3; LXVI/162 (July 14, 1904), 4; LXVI/168 (July 21, 1904), 2; LXVI/175 (July 29, 1904), 2.

17. SJN, IX/178 (August 5, 1904); IX/191 (August 19, 1904), 2; BM, LXVI/181 (August 7, 1904), 6; LXVI/185 (August 11, 1904), 2; LXVI/197 (August 25, 1904), 6.

18. BM, LXVI/203 (September 1, 1904), 2; LXVI/206 (September 6, 1904), 1; LXVI/207 (September 7, 1904), 2; LXVI/214 (September 15, 1904), 2; LXVI/221 (September 23, 1904), 2; LXVI/220 (September 22, 1904), 3; LXVI/227 (September 30, 1904), 1; SJN, IX/221 (September 23, 1904), 7.

19. BM, LXVI/238 (October 13, 1904), 1.

20. Ibid., LXVI/265 (November 15, 1904), 1; LXVI/269 (November 19, 1904), 1; LXVI/271 (November 22, 1904), 1; SJN, IX/278 (November 27, 1904), 8.

21. BM, LXVI/303 (December 31, 1904), 1.

22. Ibid., LXVII/60 (March 14, 1905), 1; LXVII/72 (March 29, 1905), 1; LXVII/78 (April 5, 1905), 1; LXVII/257 (November 8, 1905), 2.

23. Ibid., LXX/83 (April 8, 1908), 2; LXX/200 (August 25, 1908), 2; LXX/271 (November 16, 1908), 2.

24. Héctor Campos Parsi, Música, p. 224.

25. LaC, (July 14, 1909), 2, and SJN, IX/212 (September 17, 1909), 1.

26. LaC, (August 22, 1909), 1.

***

PUERTO RICO MUSICIANS

During this period (1898-1910), a number of musicians continued to compose and perform in Puerto Rico. Some of the musicians lived only a few years into the twentieth century, and although their names do not appear frequently, they nevertheless made a serious contribution, and their music was regularly performed in the first decades of the century. The first two composers, Angel Mislán, who lived just through the first decade, and Casimiro Duchesne, who lived only a few years into the twentieth century, both won considerable attention for their music.

CASIMIRO DUCHESNE (1850-1906), best known for his regional music and his orchestral conducting, was a clarinetist and member of the Artillery Band. He directed an orchestra that performed in the city parks: Borínquen and the Plaza Principal, was a guest conductor of the Police Band, and also conducted the string orchestra of the Police Band at various ceremonies in the city of San Juan. He conducted his own orchestra in various churches, in the Capilla del Cristo, in San Francisco Church for Holy Week services, and for dances during festivals in Carolina, Bayamón, and the Casino Easpañola. He won prizes for his work: in 1882, a silver medal and second class honor in the Ponce Feria Exposition for the Concert Overture, won honorable mention from the Ateneo Puertorriqueño in 1887 for another overture, in 1894 was awarded a gold medal for the same work at the San Juan Exposition during which time he also won a gold medal for his Misa a tres voces y gran orquesta, and in 1891 received a silver medal and diploma for his Sinfonía.[1]

When he conducted his orchestra he generally included music of his own. In March, 1902, in Borínquen Park, the program included works by Verdi and others, plus his danza, Un Suspiro, polka, Paquito, and mazurka, Linda.[2] In September they included works by Sousa, Isabel by Andino, and the following week played a symphony, La Mayor, and danza, La bella noche by Duchesne.[3] Their next two programs included music by Señora Cruz Verar, Andino, Bellini, and Barbieri.[4] In January, 1903, when his own orchestra played in Borínquen Park, they included his polka, La Tertulia.[5]

When he died in 1906, his orchestra continued playing without him. It was listed in the newspapers as having playing in San José Church during a novena and solemn mass in April,[6] and in June played in Borínquen Park.[7] His death was lamented by all San Juan Society.[8] The first edition of <u>Puerto Rico Musical</u>, a journal published by Arteaga, featured a critical study by Duchesne, and later in that month a benefit for the Duchesne family was given by all of the organizations in the city including the Casino Español, Ateneo Puertorriqueño,[9] Asociación de Escritores y Artistas, Amigos del Bien Público, Circulo de Amigos, La Antorcha, Juventud obrera de Santurce, Liga Social, Gremio de Torcedos, Federación Regional, Lazo de Ora, Unión Borinqueña, Federación Libre, and Derecho de Borínquen.[10] The music committee for the programs included Francisco Verar, Director of the Insular Police Band, Luis Miranda, director of the Regiment Band, and Juan Viñolo, director of the Boys' Charity School Band.

In October another benefit was given under the auspices of the Casino Español, Ateneo Puertorriqueño, La Prensa, and Sociedad de Escritores y Artistas.[11] In 1908 a project to honor Duchesne was considered. The active societies in the city, with the cooperation of the Casino Español and Ateneo, considered erecting a mausoleum on his tomb and the placing of a plaque on the house in which he had lived. This was to be accomplished by February 6, the second anniversary of his death.[12]

<u>ANGEL MISLÁN HUERTAS</u> (1862-1911) of Coamo, a prominent musician of the era, was a virtuoso performer on the euphonium, a composer of many popular danzas, and director of the band of the Tercer Batallón de Voluntarios until 1898.[1] He later became the conductor of a dance orchestra in Arecibo and a school band in Manatí. His name was not in the news very often, with the exception of when his music was performed at band concerts, but he was honored in 1909 during a festival at Manatí in the Casino Español when his waltz, <u>La Viuda Alegre</u>, was performed.[2] His danzas, <u>Sara</u>, <u>Tú y Yo</u>, <u>Pobre Borínquen</u>, and <u>Recuerdos y Lágrimas</u> have always been popular. <u>Tú y Yo</u> won honorable mention at the Buffalo Exposition in 1903,[3] and <u>Sara</u> was performed constantly by the bands in the early part of the first decade of the twentieth century and still

126

remains popular in the 1980s. The lyric character of the brief, often repeated melodies, keeps this piece in concert repertoire of present day pianists. It opens with a characteristic introductory section of eight measures which are repeated, followed by a sixteen measure section which has an introductory measure leading to the main melody, and is also repeated. (See Ex. 1)

Ex. 1 (Section A, first theme)

Then follows two sections of lyric character, each containing short melodies repeated sequentially. (See Ex. 2)

Ex. 2 (Section B)

Interesting counter melodies and a slightly chromatic character plus the contrast of staccato and legato passages makes this a rather festive piece and helped to make it a favorite with concert audiences. The work ends with an eight measure coda reminiscent of the first section of the danza proper. There are several of Mislán's works in the Archivo General de Puerto Rico but Sara is one that has been published widely in Puerto Rico as well as New York City (Spanish Music Center).

The next group of musicians lived into the second decade: Julián Andino, a brilliant performer, José Quintón, who was on the brink of an exceptional career, Fernando Callejo, who left behind him one of the finest texts on Puerto Rican music, two very prominent danza composers, Juan Ríos Ovalle and Rafael Balseiro Dávila, and Julio Carlos De Arteaga, who in spite of personal tragedy and frustrated ideals, showed great achievement especially in the field of

JULIO CARLOS DE ARTEAGA

performance. JULIO CARLOS DE ARTEAGA (1865-1923) would seem to have been born among the favored few. His Spanish grandfather, a hero in the Battle of Carabobo, married Josefina, daughter of the Marques López, and moved to Mayagüez, Puerto Rico, in 1821. Julio Carlos, born in the town of Yauco in 1865, became a second generation Puerto Rican but before his first year he was orphaned--his father, mother, and four brother and sisters died of smallpox.[1] He was adopted by a family friend, Dr. Angel Aguerevere, and Ermelindo Salizar became his godfather. Salizar would later pay the expenses of Julio Carlos' education in New York and Paris. Arteaga started his musical career on the violin at age seven, but soon changed to piano and was considered a prodigy at 13. At 14, he studied in New York with Puerto Rican pianist Gonzalo Núñez,[2] and in 1883 was accepted at the Paris Conservatoire from which he graduated in 1888 with first prize in piano accompaniment.[3] He was now prepared to conduct an orchestra, sight-read orchestral scores at the piano, and teach harmony, counterpoint, fugue, and composition.

Returning to Puerto Rico in 1888, he opened a piano and voice studio in Ponce. His pupils included Elisa Tavárez whom he prepared for the Madrid Conservatory. In 1890 he married one of his students, Nicolasa Torruella, and they moved to Havana where they lived until 1895,[4] giving recitals, and teaching piano and music theory. Among his students was Marianita Seba, later First Lady of the Republic of Cuba.

The year 1892 was a memorable one for Arteaga. He received first prize for his march Cristóbal Colón, written to celebrate the fourth centenary of the founding of America. He was also appointed music critic for El Diario de la Marina. In 1893 he was named director of the National Conservatory of Havana during the sabbatical of the permanent director, and pianist of the palace of the governor.

When Dr. Julio Henna returned from the Sorbonne in Paris, Arteaga along with Puerto Rican leaders in San Juan and Cuba met with him in New York with plans to return to Puerto Rico to organize against Spain.[5] They decided the Puerto Rican national hymn was not strong enough for soldiers to march to and from this meeting came the hymn, Libertad, with text by Félix Matos Bernier and music by Arteaga (1896).[6]

In 1900, Arteaga was appointed professor of piano and organ at the German Conservatory of Music in New York, and he gave recitals in Steinway and Mendelssohn Halls.[7] The family returned to Ponce in 1904 when Arteaga opened the Acdemia Arteaga in San Juan, and by 1905,[8] Arteaga was active in the musical culture of Puerto Rico. He presented his pupils in recital at the Ateneo Puertorriqueño,[9] performed solo concerts and participated in programs with other musicians.[10] By December, 1905, Arteaga was elected to the Board of Directors of the Association of Artists and Writers[11] and founded the Revista de Música, Puerto Rico Musical, collaborating with Braulio Dueño Colón, Fernando Callejo, Ramón Morlá, Manuel Martínez Plée, and Trindad Padilla Sanz.[12] The first issue was published in San Juan in February, 1906, and included articles on Mozart, music in New York, and noted musicians.[13] The Boletín Mercantil de Puerto Rico boasted of Arteaga's reputation in Europe and America.[14] From 1906 to 1920 Arteaga wrote music critiques for La Correspondencia de Puerto Rico. In 1906, he established his studio, Academia Arteaga, with his artist-wife Nicolasa, and taught at the Paris Bazaar.[15] Arteaga and his wife were also appointed teachers at Colegio Sagrado Corazón in Santurce.

Each year, he presented his pupils in recital.[16] He was most active in concertizing in Puerto Rico.[17] In 1907 he presented his pupils in a recital at the Ateneo Puertorriqueño.[18] The last program selection, Variations on a Theme of Beethoven by Saint-Saëns for four hands, was performed by Arteaga and Clementina Giusti. Reviews sang high praise for Arteaga and his students.[19] In April he again invited the public to hear his pupils.[20] In August, he participated in a literary-musical at the Lincoln School in a program commemorating the second anniversary of the Club Eugenio María de Hostos.[21] Monthly concerts kept him busy in 1908.[22] Accompanied at various times by his wife and pupils, he presented programs that included a wide range of international classics.

The next year was busy, too. In February, 1909, he contracted with an opera company from Curaçao to come to San Juan.[23] In the spring he organized a program in the Municipal Theatre. Taking part was Francisco Verar who was listed as honorary director and who conducted the orchestra when Arteaga played the Chopin piano concerto.[24] His pupils again performed in July and daughter, Genoveva Arteaga, performed the Haydn <u>Theme and Variations</u>.[25] Clementina Giusti sang a melody by Carlos Salcedo and a duet with Mrs. Arteaga. In October, at the Municipal Theatre, Arteaga was listed as pianist, composer, and director of the Puerto Rico Orchestra.[26] In November he and his wife gave a concert at which he played his own compositions, including <u>La Guajirita</u>, a piece of folk-song character which he composed on a text by D.H. Rosell for his wife when they lived in Cuba.[27]

Arteaga went to Santo Domingo on a concert tour in 1916. In 1917, he was invited by Alberto Williams, one of his classmates in Paris, to Buenos Aires to give a concert tour but declined because of family responsibilities. Arteaga held the position of organist and choir director at Saint John's Episcopal Church in San Juan for several years and in 1917 took the examinations of the American Guild of Organists and earned the title Associate of the Guild.

His wife died in 1918 and the next year Genoveva, her four brothers and father all returned to the states where Arteaga became organist at Saint Patrick's Cathedral in Harrisburg, Pennsylvania, where he played for one season. In 1921, Arteaga returned to New York, appointed to a position at the New York College of Music--formerly the German Conservatory of Music. That summer he and his daughter Genoveva attended the summer school at the Pius X School of Liturgical Music of Manhattanville College of the Sacred Heart in New York City.[28] Arteaga performed in concert in Caracas, Santo Domingo, Havana, and in 1922, the year before his death, triumphed in Carnegie Recital Hall in New York in May. He died September 5, 1923, and was buried in Saint Raymond Cemetary in the Bronx, New York. Julio Carlos De Arteaga's life was devoted to making music. He introduced the music of Chopin, Debussy, Cesar Franck, and Rachmaninoff to Puerto Rican audiences, and was most influential on the musical culture of the island.[29]

In May, 1979, Genoveva De Arteaga brought her father's body back to Puerto Rico for burial in San Juan. Institute of Puerto Rican Culture music director Héctor Campos Parsi was in charge of the arrangements. During the memorial mass in San Juan Cathedral, a <u>Te Deum</u> by Felipe Gutiérrez was sung by the Interdenominational Chorale of Puerto Rico. Burial followed in the San Juan Pantheon. There were concerts, a program at the Institute of Culture, and speeches praising Arteaga's career. An appropriate tribute to an outstanding musician.[30] The only piece of music in existence by Arteaga appears to be his hymn, <u>Libertad</u>, originally intended as a soldier's song. The opening section after the introduction is quoted here:

LIBERTAD

One wonders what JOSÉ IGNACIO QUINTÓN (1881-1925), Puerto Rican violinist, cellist, and composer--as highly regarded as any of his contemporaries who bridged the two centuries--might have accomplished had he not died prematurely. His father, Juan Quintón, a native of France, studied at the Paris Conservatoire and assisted the maestro de capilla of Rheims Cathedral before moving to Caguas, Puerto Rico. José Quintón composed in the style of Rossini, and remained a traditionalist throughout his short life. He departed in one work from his usual form and harmony, to explore the world of impressionism. The result was <u>Una página de mi vida</u>, a musical poem that illustrates a page of his life. Carlos Gadea-Pico, who studied with Quintón and copied much of his music, donated the work to the Puerto Rico Archives, where it is preserved in the Gadea Collection.

According to newspaper accounts of the day, Quintón's first major success came in 1911, when he won first prize in a Manatí contest for Marcha Triunfal dedicated to the memory of Josefina Parés.[1] Two years later he triumphed again in a contest sponsored by the Ponce Progressive League, with Variations on a Theme by Hummel (Variaciones sobre una tema de Hummel) and Cuarteto de cuerdas in Re Mayor (String Quartet in D Major).[2] The latter won first prize in Class A, as well as $100, a gold medal, and a diploma.[3] Other classical works by Quintón are Nocturno in E Minor (1918) and Ballade and Scherzo (1925) for instrumental ensemble. Among his principal orchestral works are Obertura de concierto, Misa de Requiem for mixed chorus and orchestra, and ten Salves for choir and orchestra.

Quintón succeeded in leaving his mark on the elegant 19th century danza by adding sections and incorporating new harmonies into the danza, and promoting it as the true expression of the island's music. For almost a quarter century, Quintón's music had lain in manuscript form, nearly forgotten. Then in February, 1973, his friends and pupils held a tribute for him at the Ateneo Puertorriqueño, during which his major works were recorded. Among those participating were Louis Antonio Ramirez, Amaury Veray, and Carlos Gadea-Pico.[4]

Quintón's danzas were pianistic in contrast to the almost Brahmsian style of his instrumental works. His danzas follow the traditional form of the earlier composers' works: introductory section, A B A , with the B section usually divided into two sections, but the melodic and accompaniment patterns are interchanged between the right and left hands making the works more challenging to the performer. Examples of Quintón's danza style may be heard on the Antología de la Danza Puertorriqueña recorded by pianist Nydia Font de Vera, Professor of music, Universidad de Puerto Rico, Río Piedras (Instituto de Cultura Puertorriqueña, Vol. 5). A review of Quintón's music summed up his qualities: he was "first among the greatest and his knowledge was the most profound and his performances showed a noble sensitivity."[5] His works showed great promise as they developed in style from the early to his last. Had he lived he would surely have been one of the most prolific Puerto Rican composers.

The year after Quintón's death, Puerto Rico lost another of its native composers. This was JULIÁN ANDINO (1845-1926), concertmaster of the opera orchestra, the orchestra of the Municipal Theatre for forty years, and the Cathedral orchestra, in which he played under the direction of Gutiérrez. His father and teacher, Domingo Andino, was the Cathedral organist for seventy years. The son appeared frequently in concerts: he played his best-known work, El Seis,[1] as a violin solo as early as June 21, 1900, during a "gran concierto vocal e instrumental" in the Theatre.[2] Then, when the legislature appropriated $10,000 to send an orchestra to the Pan American Exposition in Buffalo, Andino was one of the twenty musicians selected to represent Puerto Rico and to play native music.[3]

Andino directed a variety of instrumental ensembles that performed in concert, for benefits, and in churches. In 1903 his sextet gave a concert in the Casino Español.[4] and during Holy Week ceremonies he directed a chorus and an instrumental ensemble in San Francisco Church.[5] His band played for a bridal reception in December of 1904[6] and also furnished music for a reception to welcome the new minister and his wife at the Episcopal Church residence later in the month.[7] In 1905 his ensemble played for a children's operetta, Cinderella in Flowerland, presented in the city schools,[8] and in October, his sextet played for a ball in the Casino Español, with Joaquín Burset playing the piano.[9]

Andino was an active director, and an acclaimed violin soloist. In 1903, for instance, he was featured with a string septet at a concert in the theatre.[10] In 1907 he was featured playing the Meditation from Thaïs with an orchestra directed by Francisco Cortés.[11] He played solo violin at a Sunday concert which featured Cortés as pianist on January 25, 1907,[12] and in May he performed solo violin with an ensemble which included Manuel Tizol playing the bass violin, Prospero Marsicano on violin, J. Monclova on flute, Franz Rooms on cello, and Joaquin Burset on piano.[13] In July of the same year, Andino played under the direction of Tizol in an Ateneo concert.[14] In September and October he played in a quartet of well-known musicians--Julián Andino, Franz Rooms, Sergio Lecompte, and Manuel Tizol. Then, he performed in a sextet which included

Justo Pastor Torres on piano, Julián Andino on concert violin, Manuel Castelón on second violin, Sergio Lecompte on viola, Franz Rooms on cello, Manuel Tizol on double bass, and J. Monclova on flute.[15] They performed a String Quartet by Gonzalo Núñez at the Ateneo in October and in November, 1909, Andino, Lecompte, and Rooms played a Quartet for piano and strings by Julio Carlos De Arteaga, with the composer at the piano.[16] It appears that he also performed in an octet directed by Tizol, formed in 1909 also, with Andino as soloist.[17] The group played for banquets, celebrations, and receptions of various types.

Andino was a fine composer. One of his best known danzas was La Margarita (1870), in which he transformed the rhythm of the danza. His works were quite popular and his accompaninents were known for the "elastic rhythm," a characteristic triplet figure:

♩♪♩ or ♩♩♩
  3   3

used by danza composers, but he and Tavárez were the first to use it. When performed, the three notes are not given equal value. The first note is played faster, as if it were written : ♪♩♩ .

Andino and another leading Puerto Rican composer died in 1926. This was FERNANDO CALLEJO FERRER (1962-1926), son of a prominent nineteenth century band and orchestral director, Sandalio Callejo, wrote one of the most complete studies of music and musicians in Puerto Rico: Música y Músicos Puertorriqueños, referred to throughout this study. Callejo studied in Spain (1884-89) and returned to the island to teach piano and to compose. Music was more an avocation with Callejo. Although he cultivated the art song as well as the Puerto Rican danza and devoted a great deal of time to teaching in Ponce, San Juan, Utuado, and Manatí, he was also Postmaster in many of these towns. He had moved to Utuado in 1902 to become Postmaster as well as correspondent to the Boletín Mercantil de Puerto Rico.[1] While there he directed a chorus of young girls and children and one of their most important performances was at the Spanish Colony celebration for the feast of the Immaculate Conception.[2]

When Callejo left Utuado on April 21, 1903, to become Postmaster of Coamo, the editor of Boletín Mercantil de Puerto Rico congratulated the citizens for acquiring the "dignified and distinguished musician and composer."[3] That same year he was elected a Vice President of the Ateneo Puertorriqueño[4] The next year he was appointed Postmaster of Manatí, where he participated in a concert at the Spanish Club.[5] About once a year he was mentioned in the newspapers for his musical activities. In 1905, his zarzuela, La Cantaora, was considered for a performance by the company of Pérez Losado.[6] In 1906, he collaborated with Julio Carlos De Arteaga, Dueño Colón, Ramón Morlá, Trinidad Padilla Sanz, and Martínez Plée to found the Revista de Música, a publication consisting of essays on composers and musical trends, but which was short-lived. While in Manatí, Callejo directed a school band of twenty eight children which performed for Good Friday ceremonies, and in the fall when it played several of his own musical compositions: Ensueño y Realidad, Rosarita, two danzas, El 23 de Mayo, a vals, and a polka, Rafi. They received high praise for their performance.[7]

When it was announced that one of his danzas, Ensueño y Realidad had been published by M. Burillo & Company in San Juan, Callejo was described as an "inspired composer and notable pianist."[8] That year he also was a juror for a musical contest in San Juan.[9] The following year, his danza which had been published in 1908, was performed at a dance in the Casino Puertorriqueño in Manatí, along with his instrumental piece Deste los.[10] Over the years, Callejo's popularity keenly improved; when he visited San Juan in 1909, the Boletín Mercantil de Puerto Rico reported that "Maestro Callejo is in San Juan. He has many friends here."[11] He was Postmaster in Manatí until 1921, when embittered by politics and poverty on the island, he emigrated to New York City.

His writing appears to have been his greatest influence. As early as November 26, 1907, in La Correspondencia de Puerto Rico, he published a tribute to "El Maestro Gutiérrez," commemorating the composer's death eight years before.[12] His book, mentioned above, has not yet been surpassed and most twentieth century musical studies on the music of Puerto Rico are based on his work.

A centennial celebration of his birth was observed in 1962 with a program of his music--vocal and piano works were performed. On the program was the baritone, Pablo Elvira, who sang several of Callejo's songs accompanied by pianist Milagas Arrilaga Vicario and Nydia Font de Vera. They played Amor Silente, Mi Margarita (danza dedicated to Callejo's daughter, Margarita Callejo y Carrea, 1908), Ensueño y Realidad, and Romanza sin palabras (dedicated "a mi madre," Utuado, 1901). Introductory remarks on the significance of Callejo's works were offered by Ricardo Alegría, Director of the Institute of Puerto Rican Culture, and Amaury Veray, pianist and teacher of music at the San Juan Conservatory of Music. Several of his works are preserved in the Archivo General de Puerto Rico, some were published in New York, others remain in manuscript form, but all dating from 1889 through 1926.

Another musician of note who lived into the second decade of the twentieth century was JUAN RÍOS OVALLE (1863-1928). Ovalle was a clarinetist who succeeded Juan Morel Campos as an orchestral director of Puerto Rican danza music. Many of his compositions have been preserved in the Archivo General de Puerto Rico and some of these are dedicated to "mi amigo, Francisco Verar," the band director. Ovalle's works were often featured at band concerts and they were usually favorites with the audiences. His Graciocita (1905) was featured all through 1906 at concerts by the Police Band at concerts in Plaza Baldorioty de Castro,[1] along with his danzas, Amor Bendito,[2] and Angelina.[3] In May, 1907, the Police Band under the direction of Verar, introduced a new waltz by Rios Ovalle, Liro de Oro,[4] and in April of 1908, they introduced his new danza, María.[5] Later that year, his danza, Teresa, was awarded a prize in an Ateneo Puertorriqueño contest.[6] He also won a prize for his two-step, Bayamón, at the Lirico-literario contest in Bayamón in 1910.[7] His music was also performed that year at the Carnival in the Casino of Ponce.[8]

The regional music during this time lost much of its typical structure, and some of the more sophisticated cultivators of danzas, including Ríos Ovalle, introduced a more exotic dance structure into the form.[9] It was changed to a likeness of the North American two-step. Like Morel Campos, he conceived the danza orchestrally and many of his works followed the basic danza form: introduction followed by ABA and Coda. Like his predecessors, he achieved unity in his works by means of repeated phrases, sequences, repeated rhythmic motives, and melodic and harmonic variations. Ríos Ovalle's works, however, were more advanced harmonically than those of his predecessors, and instead of his using totally different musical material for his introductions, his brief introductory phrases lead into the first section of the danza. Also, most of the danza composers use contrasting material from one section to the next. Ríos Ovalle employed the same rhythmic figure throughout the work. For example: <u>Angelina</u>, classified as a danza, had the rhythmic figure:

♪ ♩ ♪ ♩ ♩

an augmented form of the typical rhythm:

♬ ♪ ♬ ♪

in both the right and left hand parts in each section of the work instead of presenting contrasting rhythms in the B section as in the traditional danzas. His compositional ideas were not followed by other composers, but a homage to his memory was presented in 1931 when a concert of his works was given at the Ateneo Puertorriqueño.[10]

The last of this group of composers to live into the second decade, <u>RAFAEL BALSEIRO DÁVILA</u> (1867-1929), was educated at the Jesuit College and studied music with Adolfo Heraclio Ramos. Dávila devoted his life to music and his works enjoyed a reputation comparable to that of the Viennese waltzes to which they were often compared. Balseiro Dávila's works won many prizes at home and abroad and in 1904 at the Saint Louis Exposition, he won a prize for his concert waltz, <u>El Niágara</u>.[1] It was included on a program in 1906,[2] and in January, 1907, Dávila and the Tizol orchestra played it at a concert at the Ateneo directed by Tizol.[3]

Balseiro Dávila's waltz, <u>El Cuatro de Octubre</u>, was also popular. Indeed, a special notice appeared to inform the public that it was to be performed on a program by the Police Band.[4] A reviewer stated that the work was "greatly applauded."[5] His <u>Caribbean March</u>, two step, earned similar praise, and his <u>El Niágara</u>, <u>El Cuatro de Octubre</u>, <u>Nueva York</u>, and another march, El Arribo a Guánica, were described as works of unquestionable merit.[6]

He was instrumental (with Pedro Giusti, M. Rodríguez Serra, Julio De Arteaga, Miguel R. Calderón, and Teodoro Aguilar) in forming a Philharmonic Society to promote opera productions on the island.[7] Dávila also conducted the municipal band in Manatí and they performed before the Governor.[8] He was a popular musical personality, and when he visited, The San Juan News reported about the "noted Puerto Rican pianist" who was in the city at that time.[9] One of the musicians of the Police Band, José Domínguez, dedicated a musical work to Balseiro Dávila.[10] When the artist Luisa Arregui died, he wrote a funeral march especially for the close of the ceremony.[11] One of his waltzes was performed by the Police Band in June, 1908, during a conference of professional people at the Ateneo,[12] and his danza, Teresa, won a silver medal in an Ateneo contest that August.[13] Also in September at the Ateneo Balseiro won a gold medal for his concert waltz, Puerto Rico. It was performed at a fiesta celebrating the fourth centennial of the founding of the island.[14] Following the program it was announced that the "laureate composer of Puerto Rico," Rafael Balseiro Dávila had had his waltz published by the Boletín Mercantil.[15]

In February of 1909, he won first prize at the Concurso de la Comision del Carnaval for his festive march, El Antifaz rojo,[16] and the Police Band performed it in March in Plaza Baldorioty.[17] His waltz, Floras y Perlas, was performed in Cuba in May and received accolades in the Boletín Mercantil de Puerto Rico.[18] In October, 1909, a lengthy tribute to Balseiro appeared in La Correspondencia de Puerto Rico. The musical inventiveness of Balseiro's waltzes was mentioned as the chief reason for his popularity.[19] In December, 1909, the Paris Bazaar advertised Balseiro's music for sale: concert waltz Puerto Rico, waltz from zarzuela Amor que muere y amor que nace, poetic waltz Rayo de Luz, waltz Floras y Perlas, festival march El Antifaz Rojo, and a two-step Caribe.[20] On December 21, 1909, he was elected President of the Recreativa section of the Ateneo Board of Directors for the year 1910 and was reelected for 1913 and 1916.

RAFAEL BALSEIRO DÁVILA

140

In 1914 Balseiro won a prize for a danza, <u>Una Perla</u>, one of the first danzas he composed. Curiously enough, according to his son, José A. Balseiro, the prize was a cut glass vase; a silver cup was to be awarded in the Ateneo contest for the prize danza.[21] <u>Una Perla</u> was dedicated to Manuel Tizol Márquez, director of the Municipal Band of San Juan.[22] In the same year (1914) in Ponce, he won a gold medal for a concert waltz, <u>Las Mariposas</u>, Op. 33, in a contest of the Society of Writers and Artists.[23] His works were performed by the Madrid Symphony Orchestra as well as orchestras in Puerto Rico, and in 1915, his compositions were performed by the Strand Theatre Orchestra of New York.[24] Two of his danzas, <u>Amparo</u>, and <u>Una Perla</u>, and a waltz, <u>Tus Ojos</u>, were published in New York. <u>Tus Ojos</u> is a very simple piece with a brief twelve measure introduction, three contrasting sections, and the first section repeated at the close. It has a lyric simplicity that would certainly be appealing when transcribed for band. As is evidenced by his many awards, he gained the reputation of "King of Waltzes" from his popular lilting melodies. The melody of Section A of <u>Tus Ojos</u> is given here:

One of the most notable composers of this era, BRAULIO DUEÑO COLÓN (1854-1934), native of San Juan, studied with his father, Arelio Dueño and with the Italian maestro Rosario Aruti, mentioned above. Dueño Colón was famous as a conductor, composer, author, and instrumentalist--for many years he served as first flutist in the orchestra of the San Juan Cathedral, beginning in 1880. Although books and articles on Puerto Rican music fail to mention Braulio Dueño's activities from about 1902 to 1912, he was active musically, as is evidenced by the dates of his prize-winning pieces. According to his son, Manuel Dueño, in his youth, Braulio was an extreme leftist, active in the "mojados," a secret society of "enemies against Spain."[1] He also made annual contributions to support the Cuban revotutionary forces. He was briefly imprisoned by a Spanish military Captain in the immediate aftermath of an attempt to assassinate the Captain. As Braulio approached middle age, he became a moderate and he ultimately adopted a conservative stance.

During the "transitional period" following the Spanish American War, he worked as a bookkeeper for the Palacios Company and he rode weekly from Bayamón to Toja Baja to pay the farm workers who were gathered there. In the afternoon, he was employed as a bookkeeper for Don Gerardo Soler of Santurce. When he became ill, Soler sent him to the country to recuperate; on his return, he settled in Bayamón, where he was a bookkeeper for a watch and jewelry store on San Francisco Street. There he met Gonzalo Núñez, who, when he returned to Paris, offered to finance his son's education in Paris.[2] Braulio Dueño was also active in the Masons in San Juan and was one of the principal officers elected at the dedication of the Masonic Lodge in Bayamón.[3] In December, he was elected Venerable Master[4] and must have remained active because an article in the Boletín Mercantil de Puerto Rico of 1909 mentioned him and others inviting the assembly to a meeting.[5]

Dueño Colón's music appears to have been well received at concerts and he won many prizes for his compositions, including first prize for La Amistad, an orchestral overture composed for the Ateneo contest in 1877. In 1879, he was awarded first prize for his Sinfonía de concierto for orchestra, and an Ave Maria a 4 voices and orchestra in 1882, and received honorable mention in 1887 for his Sinfonía Noche de Otoño.[6] In 1901 he won a silver medal at the Pan American Exposition at Buffalo, New York, for his Canciones escolares, dedicated to the children of Puerto Rico.[7] It was a song book for the primary grades, with texts by Fernández Juncos.[8] Canciones escolares won a gold medal and diploma in 1902 when the Puerto Rican exhibit was transferred from Buffalo to Charleston, South Carolina.[9] This shows Dueño Colón to be quite far-sighted, to have collected these children's songs. They were not all original.

The compilation included works by Beethoven, Gounod, Tchaikowsky, fragments of danzas by Morel Campos and Tavárez, and patriotic songs, America, the Star Spangled Banner, and Columbia the Gem of the Ocean with English and Spanish texts. There were forty-two songs in the first series and forty-three in the second. The book must have had quite an influence at that time because it was published in a new edition by Silver Burdett in New York in 1924 and revised by María Luisa Muñoz as Nuestras canciones in 1954.

He composed religious works for choir and orchestra, organized a municipal band in Bayamón, cultivated regional music, served as a judge for musical contests, and is mentioned in many newspaper accounts of performances of his works during the period from 1898 to 1910. Some of his works became very well known during this time and are preserved in the Archivo General de Puerto Rico: Aguinaldo Puertorriqueño, No. 1 (1898), Patria (1901), inspired by Salvador Brau's Hijo, Patria es la tierra en que se nace, for which Brau won first prize in the Ateneo contest of 1899; La Criolla (1902), Delia y Belén (1907), Rosalinda (1908), Teresa, danza for piano, Serenata Española, and a Salve for contralto and chorus which won first prize at the Ateneo contest in 1910.[10]

Evidence illustrating his popularity continues to follow him all through his life. When his Ecos de mi tierra (1892) was played by the Police Band in a concert in honor of Saint Cecilia, it was applauded so enthusiastically that the band repeated it.[11] He was chosen to be a judge of a musical contest in 1908 with Francisco Verar, Luis Miranda, Justo Pastor Torres, and Trinidad Padilla Sanz,[12] and again in 1910 was a judge of a musical composition at a fiesta with Gonzalo Núñez and Enrique Simón.[13] That year, the newspaper announced that his composition, La Criolla had been published.[14] In 1912, Dueño Colón won a contest of the Ateneo for his Liro de oro, a song he had composed for a school graduation.[15] The same year he had completed a chapter on Felipe Gutiérrez which is included in the Callejo text (Chapter 8), and in 1914, for his Estudio sobre la Danza Puertorriqueña, the Ateneo awarded him first prize, a diploma of honor and a gold bust of Juan Morel Campos.[16] That year, February 19, an article by Dueño Colon appeared in El Día (Ponce), praising the music of the composer, Arístides Chavier Arévalo.

143

Another article by him, "Los Alemanes y la música," was reprinted in <u>Cervantes</u> in 1907.[17]

Braulio Dueño Colón was a linguist, fluent in French, Italian, English, and Spanish. He wrote poetry which he published under the pseudonym, Pitirre,[18] and composed a waltz (vals brillante), <u>El Pitirre</u> which is in the Archivo General de Puerto Rico. The Colección Braulio Dueño Colón in the General Archives, donated by his daughter in 1973, contains about 200 manuscripts of music and textbooks by the Bayamón composer.

One of his compositions, <u>La Jíbara Alegre</u> is rather interesting in that it is based on the theme of <u>El Seis</u>. The dedication to Manuel Tizol, popular band conductor, most likely assured its performance at the band concerts. It includes the customary flowery introduction followed by an A section modeled after the famous theme (meas. 10-15):

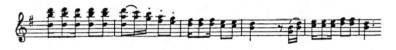

The piece is quite animated, uses sequential treatment of motives in the B section along with a contrasting section and closes with an A section.

Dueño's music is typical of the nineteenth century tradition in which he was steeped. He apparently despised the "modern" music of Stravinsky and Richard Strauss, whom he referred to as "Ricardo el pequeño."[19] When Don Pedro Giusti, proprietor of the music store, Paris Bazaar, was planning a buying trip to Europe, he asked Braulio to select music which he should bring back to his store. Until this time, the repertory of Puerto Rican pianists had consisted of fantasias arranged from operas. Braulio Dueño recommended that Giusti purchase works of Scarlatti, Clementi, Mozart, Haydn, Beethoven, Chopin--the etudes, nocturnes, mazurkas, and waltzes--and various other classical material.[20] The Giusti family embarked for Paris on May 18, 1907,[21] and returned in October of 1908.[22] Very soon this new music filtered into the concert repertoire of the artists, who found it refreshing. This transformation of musical taste of Puerto Rican performers was due to the efforts of Giusti and Braulio Dueño.[23]

144

The transformation may have taken place, but it appears from the concert programs listed in the newspapers that Puerto Rican music rather than classical music was substituted for the former opera fantasías. This was noted by Ramón Morlá in 1916 when he bemoaned the fact that the danza had taken precedence over the European masters. He was not against danza performances but he felt that there were other fine pieces which should also be heard.[24] In spite of Braulio Dueño and Pedro Giusti's efforts earlier in the century, the national spirit being what it was, danzas were always included on most of the concert programs, as they are in the 1980s.

The music of Braulio Dueño has been recorded and preserved at the Ateneo Puertorriqueño where it was performed as a homage to him on September 16, 1972, by Luis Antonio Ramírez, Isabel Gutiérrez del Arroyo, Jesús María Sanromá, Emilio S. Belaval (tenor), the chorus of the Escuela B. Dueño Colón, and the Lutheran Church Choir of Bayamón.[25]

The last composer of this group, ARÍSTIDES CHAVIER ARÉVALO (1867-1942) possessed an exceptionally promising performance background but he apparently did not participate in public concerts as did his colleagues. Although Callejo considered Chavier a "lesser" composer,[1] his works are as pianistic as most others and unlike most other composers of the era, he wrote a great deal of chamber music. Chavier studied flute and piano with local teachers in Ponce where he was born, and in 1884 he left for New York where he studied piano with the famous Puerto Rican artist Gonzalo Núñez, and harmony with Frederick Doland. He continued at the Paris Conservatoire with Georges Mathias (1886), winning many prizes and concertizing in Europe. He was greeted with great success at concerts in New York and he finally returned to Ponce in 1893.[2]

In an article announcing that he would accompany the tenor, Francisco Goicoechea, the Boletín Mercantil de Puerto Rico referred to him as a "notable pianist."[3] Chavier was praised as a "pianista de extraordinaria ejecución, [who gave a] faithful interpretation" of the masters, and his composition, La marcha triunfal, América, written for piano and band, and various string quartets and quintets, received high praise. His "exquisite artistry" was noted in these works.[4]

The next year, Chavier won first prize at the Saint Louis Exposition, receiving a gold medal and diploma of honor for a collection of seven compositions:

1. La marcha triunfal, América,
   composed for piano and string ensemble
2. Variaciones
3. Air de ballet
4. Impromptu
5. Cuarteto en Sol Mayor
6. Trio en Do Menor
7. Quinteto en Do Menor

The Puerto Rico Herald described the Puerto Rico exhibit at the Exposition and mentioned that "Young ladies from the better families in San Juan and Ponce will serve the fragrant bean [coffee] to the strains of the Puerto Rican string orchestra . . . . bordonua, tiple, bajo guitarrón," and described the music as "weird and attractive,"[5] but no mention was made specifically of Chavier's music.

Chavier was invited to adjudicate at musical contests in 1911 in Manatí, in Mayagüez in 1912, and in Ponce in 1913.[6] He apparently was also a piano teacher as in 1912 he held a recital of his most gifted pupils in a Ponce elementary school.[7] Most articles about him praised his efforts as did one by Dueño Colón on February 19, 1914, when he reviewed Chavier's string quartet in an article in El Día.

Perhaps the reason that Chavier was not as active as his colleagues who performed in concerts was that he was a leading music critic who wrote many articles about his musical contemporaries and the artistic tendencies of his age. His articles date from 1909 to 1934, and they appeared in such newspapers as The Puerto Rico Eagle (Ponce), El Día (Ponce), El Mundo, and El Tiempo. His weekly articles in El Día from 1911 to 1927 were about Puerto Rican composers, the Puerto Rican danza, European composers, including Mozart, Liszt, and Wagner, opera music, and the music of New York. His Siluetas Musicalis (1926) was a collection of these essays. His writings provided a candid view of the musical activities of this era.

The General Archives of Puerto Rico contain over seventy of his manuscripts. Among these are several works titled Variaciones--variations for the piano. One of these, Variaciones en re menor, was dedicated "A mi distinguido amigo hermano politico, Félix Matos Bernier." The work is most pianistic and reminds one of the music of Gottschalk and the flowery salón music of the earlier part of the nineteenth century. From a most simple theme as noted in the following example (meas. 1-16):

to an arpeggiated variation No. 2 (meas. 1-6):

AMALIA PAOLI

THE WOMEN WHO CARRIED ON THE TRADITION

The vitality of Puerto Rican music in a troubled time is well illustrated by the careers of three musicians--Amalia Paoli Marcano (1861-1942), Elisa Tavárez de Storer (1879-1960), and Monsita Ferrer Otero (1882-1966). Their individual efforts attest to the musical tradition begun in the nineteenth century. which was nearly smothered at the turn of the century because of the Spanish American War. The history of music in Puerto Rico in the early twentieth century is full of such quiet contributions to the island's culture. There were many women musicians, performers, teachers, and composers, but these were the most outstanding. Two concertized in Europe, the United States, and South America, and Monsita Ferrer was one of the most representative Puerto Rican composers of the early twentieth century. The performers received great publicity and Monsita Ferrer also shared fine press notices and reviews. But as a composer she was barely recognized by the press.

AMALIA PAOLI was the sister of the Puerto Rican tenor, Antonio Paoli. She was a distinguished dramatic soprano who studied in Spain and was actively singing opera in Europe before 1900. Although she enjoyed fame on foreign shores, she returned home where she made an impressive contribution to the musical world of Puerto Rico.[1] She made her debut in Madrid's Teatro Real in Aida, and when she returned home to Puerto Rico in 1904, she was immediately involved in concert life.[2] Singing first in the Municipal Theatre, she performed arias from Tosca and La Traviata with orchestral accompaniment directed by Manuel Tizol.[3] The critic of The San Juan News wrote that her low and middle registers were good, but that the principal violinist in the orchestra was too loud and she would have fared much better without the orchestra. Her aria from La Traviata was much better with the piano accompaniment of Alicia Sicardó and the reviewer reported that Amalia Paoli displayed a great flexibility of tone, her roulades were good "but her trills were generally slurred."[4] Later that year she contracted with a Mexican opera company but returned to Puerto Rico in April to sing an aria from Mefistofeles.[5] In May and June she gave concerts singing arias from Gounod's Faust, Verdi's Otello, and performing in character in zarzuelas.[6]

149

From 1904, when Amalia Paoli arrived in Puerto
Rico, until 1907 when she left for a concert tour of
the United States, she offered concerts in the
Municipal Theatre, various plazas with city bands,
and several churches. She gave concerts in San Juan,
Ponce, her native city, Coamo, and toured Caracas as
well as Cuba. She appeared with the finest musicians
and received high praise from the press. She
performed benefit concerts for the island's poor
children and later returned to concertize as well as
adjudicate voice juries for the island's music
teachers. A sampling of her performances during those
years show her virtuoso capabilities. After she
offered a concert in September, 1904, with the band
of Manuel Tizol in the Plaza of San Mateo Church in
Santurce, the critic Enrique Albacete praised her
rendition of Rossini's Tota pulchra es.[7] In
mid-October when the "distinguished soprano" offered
a "gran concierto," her program included a Romanza
from Verdi's Aida, Ave Maria, from Verdi's Otello,
and Habanera from Bizet's Carmen. The concert at the
Olimpo Hotel was under the direction of Manuel Tizol,
whose orchestra accompanied her and a chorus of
singers for the Carmen chorus which included Monsita
and Carmen Ferrer.[8] Also in October Amalia Paoli
participated in a fiesta at the Fortaleza,[9] and
sang in a zarzuela, Arte y artistas.[10] In November
she sang during a solemn mass at San Francisco Church
in Old San Juan, and under the direction of Francisco
Verar and Juan Viñolo, who directed the
orchestra,[11] she and Elisa Tavárez and others
performed during a concert in honor of Saint Cecilia
at the Ateneo.[12] She ended the year giving a
concert in her native city of Ponce in
mid-December.[13]

In October of 1905 she performed Ríos Ovalle's
zarzuela, Chateau Margaux, with Manuel Martínez Plée
in Coamo.[14] In January, 1906 she made her debut in
the National Theatre in Caracas, and apparently
performed well because a notice of her return from a
triumphant Venezuelan excursion appeared in the
news.[15] In February she participated in a
celebration given by the Governor of Puerto Rico,[16]
and a few days later was applauded after a successful
performance in Havana.[17] Again in November, she
concertized in Cuba and Santo Domingo.[18]

In 1907 Amalia Paoli was featured in several

concerts: a program in the Municipal Theatre when she was accompanied by an orchestra of forty instrumentalists directed by Francisco Cortés,[19] another program in mid-January featured her, with Cortés conducting and Julián Andino and Monsita Ferrer participating.[20] Again on March 30th, with Cortés conducting, the "simpatica diva" was scheduled to sing the role of Carmen in the Theatre, after which she received a "gran ovación" and gave a "brilliant recital."[21] In April the "diva" was scheduled to sing the first act of Carmen and a scene from the Pirates of Penzance in the Theatre.[22] On the same program she sang Elegy by Massenet accompanied by Franz Rooms, cello, and Julia Otero, piano, and sang Muerte de Margarita from Mefistofeles in character with orchestral accompaniment.[23] Late April she gave another concert with Cortés,[24] in June repeated the first act of Carmen,[25] mid-August received a rave review for a program in Coamo,[26] and September included a program in the salon of the Elks Society with all the notables: Monclova, Marsicano, Rooms, Andino, Tizol, and Burset, making up the Tizol Sextet that played an overture, accompanied the soloist and individually with Julio De Arteaga, pianist played several solos.[27] In October she sang in a benefit concert for the Society for the Protection of the Poor. Apparently her aria from the opera La Favorita by Donizetti was a favorite because she repeated it at another festive program later in the month.[28] On October 31, 1907, it was announced in the Boletín Mercantil de Puerto Rico that Amalia Paoli would embark on November 5th for the United States.[29]

Another family performer, a disciple of the important nineteenth century Puerto Rican composer, Juan Morel Campos, was the daughter of Manuel Gregorio Tavárez, ELISA TAVÁREZ (1879-1960). She studied briefly with her father until his death in 1883, and she then changed to violin, studying with Antonio Egipciaco. She returned to the piano in 1885 when she began he studies with Morel Campos. At age eight she made her debut playing the Mozart Piano Concerto in A Major with an orchestra under the direction of her teacher, Juan Morel Campos, in the Teatro La Perla in Ponce.[1] She also studied with José Galvan and when he left for Europe she continued her studies with Julio Carlos De Arteaga and harmony with Arístides Chavier. She gave frequent concerts in

151

San Juan and received a scholarship (1897) from the Provincial Governor of Puerto Rico to study for two years at the Real Conservatorio de Música in Madrid. While there she performed for the Queen María Christina, Regent of Spain who later appointed her Royal Pianist to the Court of Spain, an honor she retained for several years.[2] After graduation she studied with Isador Phillippe in Paris. She had expected to return to Puerto Rico but news of the war was so exaggerated in Spain that it led her to believe that conditions were much worse than they really were.[3] When she did return to Puerto Rico in the fall of 1899, she presented a series of concerts which brought rave reviews from the press. She became known for her interpretation of Chopin which she played with "the mastery of a consumate pianist."[4] Her program for the Women's Aid Society of Ponce,[5] for the Casino Española,[6] and for the Cadeleria fiesta in Mayagüez,[7] were all given "in her usual polished style."

By the following April she decided to open a studio in her home, 27 San Francisco Street in Old San Juan, and she advertised in the newspapers for pupils of piano and music theory.[8] A lengthy poetic tribute to her by José A. Machiavelo of Arecibo was published in a newspaper in early June. Machiavelo had become enamored of Elisa's performances and he exclaimed that they were "exquisite . . . full of life . . . brilliant . . . electrifying interpretation . . . the heart of an artist . . . a gentle pianist . . . who brings glory and honor to the people of Puerto Rico."[9] In July she was again performing Chopin in the Municipal Theatre[10] and later played Spanish airs during a ball in the casino.[11] Her "debut in public in Puerto Rico has made her a friend of music lovers."[12] Later that month she played a Fantasía by Liszt on music from Rigoletto, March Redención by her father, Mandolinata by Saint-Saëns, the Seis de Andino for piano and violin (Manuel Janer, violin), and the Liszt Rhapsody No. 12.[13] That summer she made a concert tour of the United States[14] and by fall of the year she was well established as a performer of piano music, especially that of Chopin and her father, Manuel Gregorio Tavárez.[15]

The next year she played a benefit for the women's exhibit at the Buffalo Exposition[16] and in May left for Buffalo with her mother to play several

152

concerts throughout the States.[17] When they returned she opened a studio in Arecibo.[18] She gave a concert in the Municipal Theatre[19] and was now well established as a performer and a large portrait of her appeared in The Puerto Rico Herald.[20] After her marriage to David Storer Dalmau, she moved to San Juan where she opened a studio[21] and participated with other notable performers on various occasions such as a concert in the Ateneo to celebrate the feast of Saint Cecilia.[22] She was an active member of the Ateneo and participated in concerts with the celebrated artist, Ana Otero,[23] and Cuban violinist, Claudio Brindis de Salas.[24] She also performed in various towns on the island.[25]

The Archivo General de Puerto Rico possesses several of her scrapbooks with clippings of reviews of her many performances, and programs of concerts in La Perla, Ponce, El Casino, Mayagüez, and concerts of the Banda de Bomberos playing her father's music.

For a period of time from 1911 to 1916, she dedicated herself to her three children and retired from the music world.[26] In 1917, she made five recordings for the player piano for the Aeolian Company for which she was paid $100.[27] The five pieces were Sara by Angel Mislán, Alma Sublime and Laura y Georgina by Juan Morel Campos, Sevillevas by Joaquín Taboada, and Margarita by Manuel Gregorio Tavárez. In December, 1917, Elisa Tavárez made her debut in Aeolian Hall, New York, playing a program that a music critic of The New York Times stated

"would tax the powers of almost any pianist, even outside the Antilles. Bach's Chromatic Fantasy and Fugue, Beethoven's Appasionata Sonata, a set of variations by Chopin that pianists generally leave alone, his Andante Spianato and Polonaise that have fallen out of modern programs, and Liszt's Hungarian Rhapsody No. 8."[28]

An article from the Herald stated that

"It was a dazzling performance. As an example of sheer virtuosity it was a feat, done with great ease. She plays with clarity and with musical tone. On the interpretive side, her performance leaves much to be desired. She lacks poise and does not

153

ELISA TAVÁREZ SEATED IN THE CENTER, SURROUNDED BY HER PUPILS

completely grasp the intellectual import of the composition."[29] [Refering to the Beethoven work.]

She was, however, applauded by the two world famous pianists Ignaz Jan Paderewski and Leopold Godowsky.[30]

Numerous clippings concerning her own programs and those of her pupils dated from 1924 through 1932 illustrate the fact that she was clearly one of the leading figures in Puerto Rican music. She continued her concerts in the Municipal Theatre, accompanied the violinist Andrés S. Dalmau (1921),[31] performed on the radio (Station WKAQ),[32] gave a concert at the Fortaleza,[33] and performed under Jesús Figueroa's direction, a concert with the Municipal Orchestra of forty musicians at the Ateneo.[34] She also gave many recitals of her pupils at the Ateneo.[35]

She appeared in concert with Jesús María Sanromá and Narciso Figueroa with the Puerto Rico Symphony Orchestra.[36] She performed the Schumann Piano Concerto in A Minor and Weber Konzertsteuck, Op. 79, and Sanromá and Figueroa played the Saint-Saëns Carnival of the Animals, under the direction of Augusto Rodríguez, conductor. There were other performances with the Symphony, in 1934, under the direction of Jesús Figueroa, Elisa Tavárez played the Chopin Concerto in E Minor.[37] When she visited her daughter in Marblehead, Massachusetts, The Marblehead Messenger announced Elisa Tavárez, a "world renowned pianist" would be performing and stated that "many do not realize that this concert will attract national notice, with patrons of music coming from far and near to our little town . . . . The significance is s great as if H.G. Wells had chosen Marblehead to open his lecture tour, or if Notre Dame had selected our gridiron to play Army. More power to the Marblehead Arts Association."[38] The program which included a Bach Prelude and Fugue, Beethoven Appasionata Sonata, Chopin Etude, Andante Spianato, Polonaise, Nocturne, and Scherzo, Op. 31, and Albeniz Triana.

Elisa Tavárez exerted a great influence on the musical culture of her country, and in 1950 the city of Ponce paid tribute to her. In 1954, the Ateneo Puertorriqueño paid homage, and in 1956 during music week, the celebration was dedicated to her and the memory of Juan Morel Campos. Ponce pronounced her a "favorite daughter" and San Juan declared her their "adopted daughter of the city."[39] In 1957, when the Instituto de Cultura Puertorriqueña presented a festival of Puerto Rican danzas commemorating the 110th anniversary of the birth of Juan Morel Campos in Town Hall, New York, Elisa Tavárez was a featured performer.[40]

One of the reviewers stated that

"the spontaneous applause which she won following each of the pieces she interpreted, was not the plain expression of thanks, but the heartfelt expression of enthusiasm and admiration."[41]

MONSITA MONSERRATE FERRER (1882-1966) began her piano studies at the age of six with Rosa Sicardó. She studied next with Ana Otero who had just returned from Europe.[1] She also studied with Julio Carlos De Arteaga, Arístides Chavier, and Gonzalo Núñez in New York,[2] and continued later at the Conservatorio de Música de Puerto Rico with Jesús María Sanromá.[3] She participated in concerts from 1904 on, performing in choruses from operas and presenting piano solos in the Municipal Theatre,[4] the Ateneo Puertorriqueño, and various places around the island. She served as accompanist to violinist, Angel Celestino Morales and by 1908 was referred to as a "notable" pianist.

She also won many prizes for her compositions. In 1908, a bronze medal from the Ateneo was awarded for her Vals Ideal.[5] In 1910 in Bayamón, she was given honorable mention for her North American two-step, Apolo,[6] and in 1913 or 1914 in a contest of the Sociedad de Escritores y Artistas of Ponce, she won first prize for a Nocturne in E flat Major, her last composition.[7] At that time she also won honorable mention for her danza, Ensueño de Gloria in a contest of the Sociedad de Escritores y Artistas del País.

In an article devoted to Monsita Ferrer, Amaury Veray considered her "a symbol of our tradition, our most genuine advocate, a symbol of our true heritage,"[8] and yet earlier reviewers neglected her. Veray lists among her best works: Cuarteto de cuerdas, Polonesa, Estudio en Do for piano, and her

156

most ambitious work, <u>Variaciones en la menor, sobre</u> <u>un tema de A. Chavier.</u>[9] The <u>Variaciones</u> which includes ten variations for piano is a most difficult but very pianistic work. The variations for the most part, follow closely the 24 measure theme and each variation with the exception of numbers 7 and 10 have 24 measures. The work moves through various major and minor keys: C, A, f minor, a minor, and from a rather subdued theme to an allegretto, a marcha funebre, vivace scherzando, romanza, and ending with an allegro brillante.

María Luisa Muñoz, for her Festival de Navidad, 1953, published a collection of <u>Canciones de Navidad</u> which includes a lovely <u>Pastorcillo</u> by Monsita Ferrer.[10] The work follows the regular song form (AABA) and is one of the most singable pieces in the collection.

In her danzas she has captured the singing style of the popular form. In <u>El Cuatro de Mayo</u>, after a 16 measure introduction, the A section has a <u>cantabile</u> melody with a syncopated figure in the accompaniment. Her danza, <u>Recuerdos del Pasado</u> (1966) is quite a tantilizing piece of music. After a full 16 measure introduction, not the usual 8 measures repeated, which itself has a climatic section, and the opening figure of the introduction:

is used in inversion:

to introduce the A section, which has a simple lyric melody, as pleasing as any written by her male counterparts. The typical danza triplet motive is not used but her use of syncopation in the accompaniment:

the constant repetition of motives, and modulation through various keys in section B, and the transposition of material, gives the piece a strong structural unity. There are harmonic changes that are refreshing making the work a most pleasant listening piece.

Monsita Ferrer's compositions and the performances of the two women mentioned above demonstrate a persistant attitude and an agressive spirit enabling them to be noticed and shows them to be as active as any other musician of the early decades of the century.

The last two musicians to be considered here, Ramón Morlá and Jesús Figueroa, each exerted a major influence on the musical life of the island. RAMÓN MORLÁ TRENCHS (1875-1953) arrived in Puerto Rico as a young artist at the turn of the century from his native Spain,[1] and would carry the tradition of the instrumental ensemble of the churches into the 20th century.[2] Morlá's father, Ramón Morlá Yllopsis, composer and organist of the Santa Rosa Cathedral in Barcelona, had become widowed, then entered the priesthood. Young Ramón started his career at 12 years of age as a singer in the seminary, undergoing throat surgery to enable him to reach high pitches. At the Liceo in Barcelona he studied voice and learned sacred music and composition from José Rivera Miro, a noted Spanish musician. He moved to Ponce, Puerto Rico, in 1896, a year-and-a-half before the start of the Spanish American War. A Corporal in the Spanish Army--the mounted Guardia Civil of Ponce--he remained there a year or two after the war ended, surviving by making liquor, soap, and perfume. After moving a number of times, he finally settled in San German where he married Ricarda Espiniero Pubill. In 1905, he wrote his first zarzuela, El Artista, with text by Manuel María Ramirez. In 1909, a son, Ricardo was born, and the family returned to Ponce. Morlá became conductor of the school band there as well as professor of music and band director at Juana Díaz. Already highly regarded as a musician, in 1906, he collaborated with Julio Carlos De Arteaga and other distinguished musicians on the Revista de Música, Puerto Rico Musical. That year he also composed Misa Agustiniana a 3, and the following year, Salve Regina.

In 1910, he was hired as a band director at Yauco, where he moved two years later. The following year, he became professor of music and director of the public school band, and remained there 17 years. In 1913 he served on a jury of a contest held by the Ponce Progressive League, along with Dueño Colón of Bayamón, Arístides Chavier of Ponce, Juan Ríos Ovalle, Justo R. Rivera, and José M. Morales.[3] An article by Chavier praises him as a juror of the contest and describes him as an eminent harmonist, composer, and director of the Mayagüez orchestra.[4] That same year he composed the words and music to two zarzuelas--Los Frascasados and El Bombero.

In January, 1914, he was awarded first prize by

RAMÓN MORLÁ

the Society of Writers and Artists of the Ateneo for his <u>Misa Carmelitana a</u> 4 (STTB) for orchestra and organ. Dated 1905, it was orchestrated in 1914 for the contest. Information about the Ateneo contest is written in Morlá's hand on the manuscript. Two months later, the Society of Artists and Writers of Ponce awarded him first prize for his march for band, <u>Surge et Ambula</u>.[5] Félix Matos Bernier wrote Morlá of his triumph and invited him to conduct the work at the celebration. The prize was a clock with bronze figures of a man and woman holding a sheet of music.

Morlá established a quartet that played for silent movies, operas, and zarzuelas. He played the piano, Alberto Torres, violin, Carlos Bacero, flute, and Antonio Quirós, cello. Around 1920, Ricardo Morlá was an apprentice violinist with the quartet, and Ramón's daughter, Angelina, played the piano. Ramón Morlá taught piano, harmony, composition, organ, cello, and also gave classes at the Seminario Conciliar in San Juan. A Spanish zarzuela company that traveled to Yauco performed one of Morlá's zarzuelas under the direction of Spaniard Domingo Delgado. The Yauco and Guánica theatres gave special religious concerts during which his works were performed. His ensemble often performed. with Ricardo on violin, Angelina on piano, and Ramón on cello. He directed music at Holy Rosary School in Yauco and composed formal music as well as zarzuelas for its graduation exercises. The 1918 program shows that he conducted the school orchestra, while graduates sang his <u>Welcome Song</u>. They also performed his zarzuelas <u>Quinteto de músicos Lisiados</u> and <u>Travesuras de Estudiantes</u>. In 1919, he zarzuela, <u>El Diploma</u> was performed, with Angela and Rafael Morlá taking part. In June, 1920, his zarzuela, <u>Soñar Despierto</u> was performed with Ricardo Morlá and Angelina, who also gave one of the two valedictory addresses. In 1925, they again sang his <u>Welcome Song</u> and performed his zarzuela, <u>El Ultimo Ensayo General</u>, in which Rafael and Angelina performed. From 1918 to 1920, special performances were offered at San Germán during Easter Week services. His <u>Las siete palabras de Cristo a</u> 4 for soloists, chorus, and orchestra, was performed. The choir numbered 80 and the orchestra about 40. Morlá conducted from the organ.

In July, 1926, the Morlá's moved to San Juan where he became organist of Old San Juan Cathedral, remaining there until 1940. He established the Santa

Cecilia School of Music in San Juan and directed a school band which--except for one second prize--always won first prize. In 1926 he was one of the founders of the Puerto Rico Symphony Orchestra. Morlá played violoncello, second desk, and served as secretary of the 60-piece orchestra. He was also organist at San José Church, Church of San Vicente de Paul and San Jorge in Santurce, and taught private lessons. During his tenure at the Cathedral, he directed for special occasions, an instrumental ensemble and a choir of 30 to 40 singers. Every Good Friday his choir and instrumental ensemble performed his Las siete palabras de Cristo, which was broadcast all over the island. Choirs in Caracas, Venezuela, and Medellin, Columbia, also performed the work.

Morlá was examiner for scholarships funded by the Puerto Rican government. In 1927, he judged a competition to send a student to the Royal Conservatory of Madrid. Leonor Figueroa won and was the first person from that contest to go to Spain. That year Morlá was quite productive, composing Misa de Santa Teresita del Niño Jesús a 2, Ave Maria a 2, Ecce panis a 2, and Tantum ergo a 2. Morlá was active in the Ateneo Puertorriqueño. In 1933, He and Rafael Oller were highly praised as directors of one of the zarzuelas produced that year.[6] He was also Secretary of the Ateneo that year. In the following years, Morlá composed works for string ensembles--Ante la Alhambra for quintet in 1934, String Quartet in 1943, and Entrasa y Ofertorio for string quartet, flute, clarinet 1 and 2, and trumpet.

After Morlá had left the Cathedral, in 1945, Miguel Bernal Jiménez, Secretary of the Commission of Sacred Music in Morelia, Mexico, invited him to submit some of his works, along with those by native-born Puerto Ricans for the liturgical celebrations of the month-long festival of Our Lady of Guadalupe.[7] Morlá, a master of chant, incorporated it into his compositions. Various well-known chants in modern notation are among the music copied in his hand in his collection of works. His private collection in Hato Rey, Puerto Rico, includes manuscripts and scores for church, band, orchestra, and string quartet. There are piano music, secular songs, choruses, and zarzuelas. Among his church music are hymns, litanies, gozos, salves, and a requiem. He wrote about sixteen masses for two, three, and four voices with organ and orchestra. Many of his works are orchestrated.

Morlá devised guitar methods and wrote a harmony course. He composed popular string quartets and one classical string quartet. Among his works are fugues, polkas, and waltzes, the latter dedicated to such movie stars as Mary Pickford. Perusal of his music shows that he carried on the operatic influence of the last century into the twentieth century. Morlá arrived in Puerto Rico as a young European artist, a fine organist, who also carried the instrumental ensemble tradition of the churches into the first decades of the twentieth century. Ramón Morlá was a most unusual figure. Amaury Veray wrote this tribute to him:

"He is equal to Quintón, who adopted the ways of his adopted country collaborating with island composers using their native medium, he created authentic Puerto Rican music. His solid musical preparation at the Conservatory in Barcelona permitted him to work with out rustic themes and folk music in addition to the European forms as is seen in his Aires de la montaña, Mosaicos Puertorriqueños, and his variations on the seis chorreao . . . . His tryptych of danzas, La santa María, La Pinta, and La Niña merit study and analysis from our musicians. . . they merit being known by this present generation."[8]

Composer, orchestral director, and father of one of the most celebrated musical families in Puerto Rico, JESÚS FIGUEROA IRIARTE (1878-1971) exerted an exceptional musical influence in Puerto Rico; in 1960, the Instituto de Cultura Puertorriqueña honored him with a gold medal for his devotion to the field of music and his life-long promotion of Puerto Rican music. Jesús Figueroa began his musical studies at the age of eight with José Lequerica in Aguadilla, making his debut a year later as a clarinetist.[1] After his marriage in 1902 to pianist Carmen Sanabia (1882-1954), the Figueroas moved to San Sebastian where he was director of the municipal band. They moved several times until they finally settled in San Juan (1918) and regardless of where they were located, their musical activities were recorded in the newspapers. For example, his band played in the plaza in San Sebastian,[2] his wife accompanied the violinist, Angel Celestino Morales in a concert in

Lares,[3] Mrs. Figueroa performed at a literary-musical under the auspices of the Club Eugenio María de Hostos at the Lincoln School.[4] She played a Godard Mazurka and accompanied violinist Sr. Dulievre. From San Sebastian they moved to Aguadilla, spent time in Santo Domingo where Jesús founded a military band of the Ozama Battalion, and returned to San Juan where he was appointed director of the municipal band in Río Piedras (1909).[5] That August he directed the band in a program in the theatre in Río Piedras. The program was dedicated to the teachers of the normal school and the program included scenes from zarzuelas.[6]

In 1918, Jesús Figueroa moved his family to San Juan where he established a music studio and formed a municipal band and orchestra.[7] He directed both ensembles and concentrated on the performance of Puerto Rican music. From 1920 to 1927 he also conducted the National Guard Band. During this time, in 1925, he conducted an orchestra of forty members at a concert in the Theatre which featured Jaime Figueroa Sanabia, violin, and Elisa Tavárez, pianist, both playing several selections. Jesús Figueroa was a founder of the Puerto Rico Symphony Orchestra, an elected member of the Board of Directors of the Orchestra, and a composer of danzas, zarzuelas, operas, and shorter vocal works. In the latter group is a lovely song, Villancico del Nacimiento included in the Muñoz Canciones de Navidad collection. After an introductory four measure phrase, the song is a delight.

Jesús Figueroa's works are preserved in the Figueroa private library in the family home. Three of his compositions are in the Archivo General de Puerto Rico: Nobleza, a piece for flute, clarinet in C, trombone, violin, viola, cello, and bass, apparently written at the time of the "Ciclón de San Felipe, September, 1928," and Himno de Lares are in the Eduardo Franklin Collection, and a danza, La Danza Nueva (1938) is in the Monserrate Deliz Collection. In 1968, a concert in honor of Jesús Figueroa was presented at the Ateneo which has preserved it on tape.[8] All of his children are world-renown musicians and are discussed in the concluding chapter.

Chapter VII Notes

1. Casimiro Duchesne Notes

1. Cortijo, pp. 416–17, and Callejo, pp. 200–1.

2. BM, LXIV/62 (March 15, 1902), 1.

3. Ibid., LXIV/211 (September 11, 1902), 3, and SJN, VII/303 (September 19, 1902), 3.

4. BM, LXIV/222 (September 25, 1902), 1, and SJN, VII/311 (September 28, 1902), 5.

5. BM, LXV/6 (January 8, 1903), 8, and LXV/14 (January 17, 1903), 2.

6. Ibid., LXVIII/94 (April 23, 1906), 2.

7. Ibid., LXVIII/146 (June 22, 1906), 2.

8. Ibid., LXVIII/31 (February 6, 1906), 1.

9. Ibid., LXVIII/37 (February 12, 1906), 2.

10. Ibid., LXVIII/44 (February 21, 1906), 3.

11. Ibid., LXVIII/218 (September 15, 1906), 2, and LXVIII/248 (October 20, 1906), 2.

12. Ibid., LXX/71 (January 21, 1908), 2, and LaC, (February 8, 1908), 3, and (March 30, 1908), 2.

***

2. Angel Mislán Notes

1. Carlos N. Carreras. Hombres y mujeres de Puerto Rico. México: Orión, 1957, p. 160.

2. LaC, (December 14, 1909), 2.

3. SJN, VI/230 (October 3, 1901), 1, and VI/238 (October 12, 1901), 7. Honorable mention also went to Juan Morel Campos of Ponce (posthumously) for his march, Juegas florales, which had been sent to the Exposition as an example of Puerto Rican music.

***

3. Julio Carlos De Arteaga Notes

1. When Julio Carlos' godfather arranged for his legal papers so
   that he might go to Europe to study, the godfather found
   that because of fires in the church, there was no registry
   of births. He therefore, stated that Julio was born in 1867
   in Ponce, but according to Genoveva De Arteaga, he was born
   in Yauco in 1865.

2. Euterpe [Organo Oficial de la Sociedad Amigos de Arteaga,
   Inc.], (May 6, 1972, 4, stated that Arteaga studied with
   Horatio Parker as well as with Núñez in 1882. It was after
   his European studies, however, that he took a few lessons
   from Parker in New York.

3. Certificado de mérito, 1888—Julio Carlos Eduardo Arteaga,
   first prize in piano accompaniment from the Conservatoire
   National Superieur de Musique, Paris—is in the Archivo
   General de Puerto Rico.

4. The Arteaga family included six children. The first, Angela,
   was born in 1897, lived only a few hours. She was followed
   by Genoveva in 1898, and then by four boys—Pedro in 1902,
   Julio Carlos in 1907, Jorge in 1911, and Diego in 1913.

5. Genoveva De Arteaga, "La Historia de un Himno Revolutionario
   de mis impresiones de La Habana," Carteles, n.d., n.p.

6. Ibid.

7. "Los grabados de este numero," n.d., n.p., no name of
   newspaper, in the file at the Archivo General de Puerto Rico.

8. Muñoz, p. 116, claims that he returned to Puerto Rico in 1920
   when he established an academy of music in Río Piedras. The
   BM, LXVII/84 (April 12, 1905), 1, states that he established
   an academy of music and at that date was to appear at the
   Ateneo.

9. BM, LXVII/217 (September 16, 1905), 6.

10. Ibid., LXVII/235 (October 13, 1905), 1.

11. Ibid., LXVII/283 (December 9, 1905), 1.

12. Callejo, p. 82. There was also an announcement in the BM,
    LXVIII/36 (February 12, 1906), 2, and on February 15,
    concerning the Revista, and El Mundo, (September 15, 1923),
    Archivo General de Puerto Rico Reference Room, Vol. 5, n.p.,
    by Chavier.

13. Only one copy exists in the Archivo General Reference Room. Mrs. Arteaga advertised in the journal (p. 11), that she taught lessons in elementary theory, solfeo, piano, and all levels of singing at 27 San Francisco Street.

14. BM, LXVIII/42 (February 17, 1906), 7.

15. Ibid., LXVIII/8 (January 10, 1906), 1. His studio was in the front and the family--two aunts, a cook, parents, and children occupied the rest of the seven rooms.

16. Ibid., LXVIII/121 (May 24, 1906), 6.

17. Ibid., LXVIII/300 (December 20, 1906), 7.

18. Ibid., LXIX/9 (January 11, 1907), 2.

19. LaC, 17 (January 12, 1907), 3.

20. BM, LXIX/85 (April 13, 1907), 2.

21. LaC, 17 (August 10, 1907), 1, and BM, LXIX/188 (August 10, 1907), 2.

22. BM, LXX/13. (January 16, 1908), 2; LXX/47 (February 25, 1908), 7; LXX/70 (March 23, 1908), 2; LXX/178 (July 31, 1908), 2; LXX/208 (September 3, 1908), 2; LXX/226 (September 24, 1908), 2; LXX/266 (November 10, 1908), 2; LXX/267 (November 11, 1908), 2, and LaC, 18 (January 17, 1908), 2; (January 24, 1908), 4; (February 26, 1908), 2; (February 27, 1908), 2; (April 29, 1908), 2; (May 16, 1908), 2; (June 4, 1908), 1.

23. BM, LXX/277 (December 18, 1908), 2.

24. Ibid., LXXI/49 (February 27, 1909), 2; LXXI/68 (March 24, 1909), 3, and "Julio C. Arteaga," Euterpe, (December. 1972), n.p., stated it was the first but the BM, LXVII/224 (September 30, 1905), 4, lists an earlier performance but does not name the artist.

25. LaC, 19 (July 4, 1909), 2.

26. BM, LXXI/240 (October 4, 1909), 3, and LaC, 19 (October 7, 1909), 2, and (October 10, 1909), 7.

27. BM, LXXI/274 (November 13, 1909), 3. (Guajirita refers to Cuban country folk. This song is of folksong character.)

28. Genoveva De Arteaga in an interview, July 1, 1976, said that the Wards gave her father a German edition of the works of Chopin when they left San Juan, and she recalled Justine Ward as being in a state of shock that summer over her broken marriage which had ended in an annulment in 1919. The Catholic Choirmaster, VII/4 (October, 1921), 120, includes a picture of J.C. Arteaga.

29. Euterpe, (December, 1972), n.p.

30. "A Tribute to Julio C. De Arteaga," a complete issue of Revista Euterpe, VIII (October/November, 1979), is dedicated to Arteaga and gives all details of the mass, concerts, and programs in his honor given in Puerto Rico in May, 1979.

***

4. José Ignacio Quintón Notes

1. "La Marcha de un Quintón," La Democracia, (May 27, 1911). Archivo General de Puerto Rico Reference Room, Vol. 6, n.p. The original manuscript, dedicated to Josefina Parés, is in the Archivo General, No. 1430.

2. "El Gran Certamen Musical," The Puerto Rico Eagle, (October 24, 1913), Archivo General Reference Room, Vo. 1, n.p. The original manuscript is in the Carlos Gadea Collection with a photograph of the diploma. The ms has "Beethoven es el maestro de los maestros," written on the opening leaf, but the work appears to be more reminiscent of Schubert.

3. The Puerto Rico Eagle, ibid.

4. One and a half hours of tape, Nos. 73–74.

5. J.A. Burset, "La Danza Puertorriqueña en el Ateneo," LaC, (January 31, 1931), 4, Archivo General file.

***

5. Julián Andino Notes

1. Also known as the Seis de Andino, Seis chorreao. (San Juan, P.R.: José Laza & Co., 1910). The seis continues to be danced in the country, especially during the nativity season. (See Muñoz, La música en Puerto Rico, pp. 46–49.) Héctor Campos Parsi, contemporary Puerto Rican composer, has used the theme of the seis in his Sonata in G for piano. (New York: Peer International: Cook Recording No. 1961, Jesús María Sanromá, pianist.

2. Diario de Puerto Rico, I/142 (June 20, 1900), 4.

3. SJN, VI/14 (January 17, 1901), 2; According to ibid., VI/43 (February 20, 1901), 5, the Paris Bazaar offered a free trip to the person who made the most purchases at the Paris Bazaar between February 1 and May 1; Also see ibid., VI/73 (March 30, 1901), 3; and VI/230 (October 3, 1901), 1, and VI/237 (October 11, 1901), 1, Puerto Ricans were awarded a total of 153 prizes: ten gold medals for coffee, tobacco, and cigarette exhibits, 16 silver medals and 45 bronze medals were awarded to the cigars, cigarettes, rum, and coffee exhibits. Also see BM, LXVIII/69 (March 23, 1901), 2, and El País, VII/56 (March 7, 1901), 3, and VII/75 (March 29, 1901), 2.

4. BM, LXV/74 (March 30, 1903), 2.

5. Ibid., LXV/80 (April 6, 1903), 3.

6. SJN, IX/295 (December 17, 1904), 1.

7. Ibid., IX/301 (December 24, 1904), 8.

8. BM, LXVII/60 (March 14, 1905), 2.

9. Ibid., LXVII/225 (October 2, 1905), 4.

10. SJN, VIII/161 (July 17, 1903), 5.

11. BM, LXIX/11 (January 14, 1907), 2.

12. Ibid., LXIX/22 (January 26, 1907), 7.

13. Ibid., LXIX/104 (May 3, 1907), 2.

14. Ibid., LXIX/59 (July 8, 1907), 2.

15. Ibid., LXIX/222 (September 20, 1907), 2, and LXIX/235 (October 5, 1907), 2.

16. Ibid., LXXI/238 (October 1, 1909), 1, and LXX1/274 (November 13, 1909), 3.

17. Callejo, p. 72, lists a few activities for Andino before this.

***

6. Fernando Callejo Ferrer Notes

1. BM, LXIV/281 (December 16, 1902), 2.

2. Ibid., LXIV/281 (December 4, 1902), 3.

3. SJN, VIII/84 (April 14, 1903), 3, and BM, LXV/85 (April 14, 1903), 2.

4. SJN, VIII/232 (October 10, 1903), 5.

5. Ibid., IX/60 (March 12, 1904), 5.

6. BM, LXVII/72 (March 29, 1905), 1.

7. LaC, (March 27, 1907), 2, and (November 7, 1907), 1.

8. Ibid., (February 20, 1908), 2.

9. Callejo, p. 184.

10. BM, LXXI/125 (May 31, 1909), 2.

11. Ibid., LXXI/151 (June 24, 1909), 2.

12. LaC, (November 26, 1907), 2.

***

7. Juan Ríos Ovalle Notes

1. BM, LXVII/294 (December 22, 1905), 1.

2. Ibid., LXVIII/12 (January 15, 1906), 4, 7, and LXVIII/52 (March 3, 1906), 2.

3. Ibid., LXVIII/64 (March 17, 1906), 2, and LaC, (March 6, 1907), 2.

4. LaC, (May 25, 1907), 2.

5. Ibid., (April 11, 1908), 2.

6. BM, LXX/204 (August 29, 1908), 2.

7. Callejo, p. 185, and BM, LXX/127 (September 14, 1910), 7.

8. The Puerto Rico Eagle, IX/2502 (January 29, 1910), 8.

9. Compositores Puertorriqueños, p. 9, and Carmen Gómez Tejera, p. 99.

10. El Mundo, XIX/31 (January 30, 1931), 6.

***

8. Rafael Balseiro Dávila Notes

1. "Rafael Balseiro Dávila," The Puerto Rico Herald, III/145 (May 7, 1904), 1464.

2. BM, LXVIII/245 (October 17, 1906), 2.

3. Ibid., LXIX/11 (January 14, 1907), 2. El Niágara was published by José Laza & Co., March 22, 1907). A copy is in the Colección Fa. Storer-Tavárez in the Archivo General de Puerto Rico.

4. LaC, 17 (January 6, 1907), 1.

5. Ibid., (January 8, 1907), 4.

6. Ibid., (February 11, 1907), 1.

7. Ibid., (March 22. 1907), 2.

8. Ibid., (September 9, 1907), 2.

9. SJN, IX/142 (June 21, 1904), 5.

10. LaC, 17 (October 18, 1907), 2.

11. Ibid., 18 (April 21, 1908), 3.

12. Ibid., (June 6, 1908), 1.

13. BM, LXX/188 (August 10, 1908), 1, and LXX/189 (August 11, 1908), 3.

14. Ibid., LXX/229 (September 28, 1908), 2.

15. Ibid., LXX/216 (September 18, 1908), 2.

16. Ibid., LXXI/35 (February 11, 1909), 2.

17. Ibid., LXXI/60 (March 13, 1909), 7, and played again in August according to ibid., LXXI/206 (August 24, 1909), 2.

18. Ibid., LXXI/121 (May 27, 1909), 2.

19. LaC, 19 (October 24, 1909), 3.

20. Ibid., 17 (December 27, 1907), 4, and BM, LXXII/217 (September 14, 1910), 7.

21. José A. Balseiro, "Dos Danzas de Rafael Balseiro Dávila," Revista del Instituto de Cultura Puertorriqueña, VI/20 (July-September. 1963), 22. See LaC, 19 (October 23, 2909), 4, for the story of Ward presenting the silver cup.

22. José A. Balseiro, pp. 22-23.

23. Callejo, p. 188.

24. Compositores Puertorriqueños, p. 1.

***

9. Braulio Dueño Colón Notes

1. Manuel Dueño. Braulio Dueño Colón Estudio Biográfico. Bayamón: Imp. Moreno Hijo, 1944, p. 22.

2. Ibid., pp. 26-27. The offer was refused and Manuel Dueño later studied medicine in the United States.

3. SJN, VIII/121 (May 27, 1903), 3.

4. Ibid., VIII/282 (December 8, 1903), 4.

5. BM, LXXI/210 (August 28, 1909), 2.

6. Ateneo Puertorriqueño, n.p.

7. El País, VII/56 (March 7, 1901), 3; VII/189 (August 13, 1901), 3; VII/221 (September 24, 1901), 1, and SJN, VI/237 (October 11, 1901), 1.

8. El País, VII/221 (September 24, 1901), 1.

9. El País, VII/145 (June 15, 1901), 3; BM, LXIV/120 (May 24, 1902), 1; ibid., LXIII/231 (October 8, 1901), 1; SJN, VI/137 (June 13, 1901), 1; ibid., VII/103 (May 4, 1902), 1.

10. Manuel Dueño, p. 33. The Ateneo Puertorriqueño, lists no contest for 1910. The BM, LXXII/62 (March 18, 1910), 2, mentions a fiesta in which Dueño Colón and Gonzalo Núñez both acted as judges of the musical compositions for orchestra.

11. SJN, VII/271 (November 24, 1903), 8.

12. BM, LXX/184 (August 5, 1908), 1.

13. Ibid., LXXII/62 (March 18, 1910), 2.

14. Ibid., LXVIII/95 (April 24, 1910), 2.

15. Callejo, p. 100, and Callejo, "Braulio Dueño Colón," El mes histórico, I/8 (March, 1935), 7-11. The Ateneo bulletin of 1966 lists no contest in 1912. Manuel Dueño, p. 33, lists two Canciones escolares, one for graduation dated 1910 and the other Navidad was given honorable mention at the Ateneo also in 1910.

16. A copy is in the Monserrate Deliz Collection in the Archivo General de Puerto Rico, No. 52. Braulio Dueño Colón, "Estudio sobre la danza Puertorriqueña," in Brújula, III/9-10 (November, 1937), 117-121, in De semántica musical y otros estudios (Mergal Llera, ed.). Manuel Dueño cites the date as 1910. No event is listed for 1910 or 1914 in the Ateneo bulletin. A copy of his Estudio . . . exists in mimeograph form in the Archivo General de Puerto Rico, Music Archives, Braulio Dueño Colón folder, n.d.

17. Cervantes, III/17 (June 30, 1907), 424-5.

18. Manuel Dueño, p. 28. His friend, Luis Brau published a weekly column in his revista Pica Pica and Braulio sent poetry to him from Bayamón.

19. Manuel Dueño, p. 29.

20. Ibid., p. 30.

21. LaC, 17 (May 13, 1907), 3.

22. BM, LXX/238 (October 8, 1908), 3.

23. Manuel Dueño, pp. 29-30.

24. Ramón Morlá, Yauco (May 8, 1916). Archivo General de Puerto Rico Reference Room, Vol. III, no name of newspaper, n.p.

25. Tape No. CM, 72-32.

***

10. Arístides Chavier Notes

1. Callejo, p. 410.

2. Cortijo, p. 410.

3. BM, LXIV/291 (December 17, 1902), 7, and LXV/10 (January 13, 1903), 2.

4. The Puerto Rico Herald, [New York] I/26 (January 4, 1902), 1.

5. Félix Matos Bernier, Isle de Arte. San Juan: Imp. La Primavera, 1907, p. 233, and The Puerto Rico Herald, III/117 (October 24, 1903), 1012-3.

6. Callejo, pp. 186-7.

7. El Día, (September 20, 1912), Book 6, Archivo General de Puerto Rico Reference Room, n.p.

***

11. Amalia Paoli Notes

1. Callejo, pp. 171-2.

2. SJN, VIII/294 (December 22, 1903), 5, and The Porto Rico Journal, I/3 (December 29, 1903), 3.

3. SJN, VIII/300 (December 31, 1903), 4.

4. Ibid., IX/3 (January 4, 1904), 8.

5. Ibid., IX/78 (April 7, 1904), 5.

6. Ibid., IX/117 (May 21, 1904), 4, and IX/127 (June 3, 1904), 4.

7. BM, LXVI/221 (September 23, 1904), 2, and LXVI/220 (September 22, 1904), 3, and LXVI/224 (September 27, 1904), 1.

8. Ibid., LXVI/225 (September 28, 1904), 7, and LXVI/237 (October 12, 1904), 1, and LXVI/241 (October 17, 1904), 2, and SJN, IX/238 (October 13, 1904), 5.

9. BM, LXVI/251 (October 28, 1904), 2.

10. Ibid., 1.

11. Ibid., LXVI/263 (November 12, 1904), 3, and LXVI/264 (November 14, 1904), 1.

12. Ibid., 2, and LXVI/265 (November 15, 1904), 2, and LXVI/271 (November 22, 1904), 2.

13. SJN, IX/293 (December 15, 1904), 8.

14. BM, LXVII/226 (October 3, 1905), 2; LXVII/249 (October 30, 1905), 4, and LXVII/255 (November 6, 1905), 3.

15. LaC, 16 (January 11, 1906), 1, and Puerto Rico Musical, Revista de Música (Julio C. Arteaga, ed.), I/1 (February 15, 1906), 11.

16. The Puerto Rico Eagle, IV (February 26, 1906), 8.

17. BM, LXVIII/49 (February 26, 1906), 8.

18. Ibid., LXVIII/272 (November 17, 1906), 5.

19. Ibid., LXIX/11 (January 14, 1907), 2.

20. Ibid., LXIX/22 (January 26, 1907), 7.

21. Ibid., LXIX/69 (March 22, 1907), 2; LXIX/72 (March 26, 1907), 2, and LaC, 17 (April 1, 1907), 3.

22. BM, LXIX/82 (April 8, 1907), 2.

23. Ibid., LXIX/80 (April 5, 1907), 2, and LaC, 17 (April 6, 1907), 2.

24. BM, LXIX/99 (April 27, 1907), 2.

25. LaC, 17 (June 11, 1907), 2.

26. BM, LXIX/190 (August 13, 1907), 2.

27. Ibid., LXIX/222 (September 20, 1907), 2, and LaC, 17 (September 23, 1907), 1.

28. LaC, 17 (October 16, 1907), 1, and (October 19, 1907), 3.

29. BM, LXIX/257 (October 31, 1907), 2.

***

12. Elisa Tavárez Notes

1. "Elisa Tavárez Colom," Nosotros, II/1 (May/June, 1968), 15.

2. Colección Elisa Tavárez, Box No. 3, and Scrapbook "Año 1924", n.p. There is a certificate from the Queen dated 1904.

3. Elisa Tavárez Estudio Biográfico. San Juan: Departamento de Instrucción Pública, 1958, p. 4. According to an article in her Scrapbook Año 1933 in the Archivo General de Puerto Rico, she was a pianist for the Royal Court of Spain for 14 years.

4. El País, V/291 (December 12, 1899), 2.

5. SJN, IV/11 (January 9, 1900), 1, and Scrapbook "Desde 1900", p. 69.

6. SJN, IV/49 (January 31, 1900), 2.

7. Ibid., IV/61 (February 7, 1900), 1.

8. Ibid., IV/103 (March 9, 1900), 3, and Diario de Puerto Rico, I/75 (April 2, 1900), 4, and I/79 (April 6, 1900), 4.

9. Diario de Puerto Rico, I/22 (June 9, 1900), 6.

10. El País, VII/174 (July 24, 1900), 1.

11. SJN, IV/324 (July 24, 1900), 1.

12. Ibid., IV/326 (July 25, 1900), 1.

13. Scrapbook "Desde 1900".

14. SJN, V/67 (September 19, 1900), 1.

15. Ibid., V/73 (September 26, 1900), 1, and BM, LXII/286 (December 14, 1900), 2.

16. SJN, VI/74 (April 4, 1901), 4.

17. Ibid., VI/113 (May 15, 1909), 8; VI/160 (July 13, 1901), 3, and BM, LXIII/110 (May 11. 1901), 3.

18. SJN, VI/163 (July 21, 1901), 1, and VI/168 (July 23, 1901), 7.

19. El País, VII/174 (July 24, 1901), 1.

20. I/19 (November 16, 1901), 7.

21. Starting in BM, LXVI/278 (December 1, 1904), 1, she advertised throughout December on page 1.

22. Ibid., LXVI/264 (November 14, 1904), 2, and LXVI/271 (November 22, 1904), 2.

23. Veray, p. 24.

24. Ibid., This clipping is in her Scrapbook "Desde 1900," p. 47.

25. Scrapbook "Desde 1900," pp. 51, 57, 60, 61, and BM, LXVIII/207 (September 3, 1906), 2.

26. "Elisa Tavárez Colom," Nosotros, 15.

27. Archivo General de Puerto Rico, Colección Elisa Tavárez, No. 3.

28. The New York Times, (December 2, 1917), 18.

29. Scrapbook "Año 1924," p. 73, Clara T. Nichols, music critic.

30. Ibid.

31. La Democracia, (January 19, 1921), p. 74 of Scrapbook "Año 1924."

32. Scrapbook "Año 1924," p. 70, gave her life and a great tribute to her.

33. Héctor Campos Parsi, Música, Vo. VII of La Gran Enciclopedia, p. 218.

34. July 31, 1925, program in Scrapbook "Año 1924."

35. Héctor Campos Parsi, p. 125.

36. Scrapbook "Año 1924," August 28, 1932.

37. Campos Parsi, p. 231.

38. LXVI/46 (November 19, 1937) in Scrapbook "Año 1933," in the Archivo General de Puerto Rico, and Editorial, Marblehead Messenger, (November 12, 1937), 6.

39. Scrapbook "Año 1933." Veray lists her recordings (p. 25).

40. Scrapbook 1956-1959, and El Mundo, (April 22, 1957).

41. Scrapbook "Año 1958."

***

13. Monsita Ferrer Notes

1. Amaury Veray, "Monsita Ferrer," Revista del Instituto de
   Cultura Puertorriqueña, V/7 (October-December, 1962), 10.

2. Callejo, p. 202.

3. Veray, p. 10.

4. BM, LXVI/241 (October 17, 1904), 2; LXVIII/122 (May 25,
   1906), 1, and LXIX/11 (January 14, 1907), 2.

5. Ibid., LXX/188 (August 10, 1908), 1. Her work, but not
   her name, is mentioned.

6. Callejo, p. 185.

7. The dates of the contests differ between authors. Veray, p.
   10, gives the date as 1913; Callejo, p. 188, gives 1914.

8. Veray, p. 11.

9. Ibid.

10. María Luisa Muñoz. Canciones de Navidad. San Juan, P.R.
    Departamento de Instrucción Pública, 1953, pp. 17-19.

***

14. Ramón Morlá Notes

1. According to Amaury Veray. Vida y Desarrollo de la danza
   Puertorriqueña. Unpublished manuscript, n.d., Morlá arrived
   in 1898 when he was 23 years old. Ricardo Morlá, his son,
   claims that he arrived in 1896. The Baptismal Certificate
   (Parroquia de San Juan Bautista de Vals, Provincia y
   Arzobispado de Terragona. Certifico que en el Folio 368 del
   libro 32 de Bautismis) gives the date of his birth as June
   27, 1875.

2. According to Monsignor Arroyo, Rector of the San Juan
   Cathedral, the orchestral tradition died after Morlá.

3. Callejo, pp. 187-8.

4. In the Archivo General de Puerto Rico Reference Room Vol. 6,
   n.p. there is an article in tribute "A don Ramón Morlá:
   Miembro del Jurado Calificador en el Certamen de Liga
   Progresista de Ponce," Diario al Oeste [Mayagüez, P.R.],
   (November 11, 1913).

5. Dated Ponce, March 26, 1914.

6. June 5, 1933. Monserrate Deliz Scrapbooks, 1933, in the Music Collection, University of Puerto Rico, Río Piedras, p. 5a.

7. A letter from Miguel Bernal Jiménez to Morlá (April 23, 1945) in the possession of Ricardo Morlá.

8. Amaury Veray. Vida y desarrollo de la danza Puertorriqueña, p. 23

***

15. Jesús Figueroa Notes

1. Yvette Ortiz. La Canción de Arte Puertorriqueña. San Juan: Instituto de Cultura Puertorriqueña, 1975, p. 16.

2. BM, LXIV/284 (December 9, 1902), 3.

3. Ibid., LXVI/191 (August 19, 1904), 1.

4. LaC, 17 (August 10, 1907), 1.

5. BM, LXXI/183 (July 27, 1909), 3.

6. LaC, 19 (August 28, 1909), 2.

7. Muñoz, La música . . ., p. 157.

8. Ateneo Puertorriqueño, September 15, 1968, 2 hour tape (CM 68-31).

***

Although most of the books and articles on Puerto Rican music have overlooked the extensive musical activities following the Spanish-American War, this study has demonstrated that it was far from a period of cultural regression in terms of the continuation of the nineteenth century musical tradition into the twentieth century. Fernando Callejo explained that there was a relationship between the economic difficulties which followed the American takeover of the island and the cultural climate. However true that may be for other cultural forms, in the case of music, it is evident that Puerto Rico was blessed with a generation of musicians who brought the island and its people into the new century with a sense of pride, as well as a sense of nascent nationalism. Much of the music composed during the period was not published, and that fact meant that only historians who actively sought to locate manuscript material, and who examined the newspapers and other records of Puerto Rico would become aware of the intensive musical tradition of the time period.

It is clear that the most critical period in the history of Puerto Rico was the decade following the Spanish-American War, representing a major transition from Spanish and European control to control and dominance by the United States, economically, politically, and culturally, Military governors were appointed by a succession of American presidents, and the United States Army assumed control of civil and church property on the island. During that period there was a severe economic crisis which had a profound impact upon the island and its citizens. During this transition period, Puerto Rican musicians and music educators sought to preserve native music styles, while adapting to the new situation. They expanded upon the danza form, composed music which appealed to the native cultural tradition, while adding patriotic American music to their repertoire. During this period, traditional Spanish-Catholic feast days began to lose their importance, while American holidays began to be celebrated. Yet, it was clear from the beginning that the native Puerto Ricans did not want to be submerged into the dominant American culture. The early American rulers tried to transform a Spanish-speaking people into Americans, substituting English for Spanish as the official

GENOVEVA DE ARTEAGA

language, with very little regard for what they considered to be an inferior native culture. It was not until George Cabot Ward arrived on the island that the Puerto Ricans finally found that an American appointed official could be aware of and respectful to the native tradition. If we add to the cultural conflict between the Spanish and English tradition the economic problems resulting from the devastation of the hurricane of 1899 and from the new economic relationships necessitated by the American control of the island, we set the stage for the development of feelings of hostility that can be seen almost one hundred years later.

During this period, a number of excellent native musicians took center stage, developing bands which provided entertainment while at the same time strengthening the traditional mood and providing for the transition to the new world of the twentieth century, a world dominated by a colonial relationship with the United States, which clearly had assumed a position of dominance in the western hemisphere. Here we see such musicians as Francisco Verar, Luis R. Miranda, and Manuel Tizol establishing bands which continued to perform through the period under study. At the same time, Angel Mislán, Juan Ríos Ovalle, Rafael Balseiro Dávila, and Braulio Dueño Colón moved to the fore as leading Puerto Rican composers, providing much of the music for a land facing a major transition, indeed a cultural revolution imposed upon by the new political situation.

Finally, it is important to note that many of the musicians who provided cultural leadership during the decade following the Spanish-American War had far-reaching significance which continued into the modern period, not only through their music, but also through their sons and daughters, the products of this period of transition. An outstanding example is GENOVEVA DE ARTEAGA, the daughter of Julio Carlos De Arteaga. Genoveva was born in 1898, and began her musical training under the tutelage of her parents, studying at the Academia Arteaga in Santurce.[1] At an early age she was reported to play works for four-hands on the piano, with her father. From 1909 to 1913, she studied at the College of the Sacred Heart in Santurce, and from 1917 to 1920 she became a piano teacher at the College.[2] In 1921, at the age of 23, she went to New York where she studied at the New York College of Music, and at the Guilmant Organ

School where she held a Philip Berolzheimer scholarship. While in New York, she performed a recital at the Waldorf Astoria for the Spanish-American Association, studied at the Pius X School of Liturgical Music (Manhattanville College), and graduated with honors from the New York College of Music (1922).[3] On June 16, 1922, she presented a graduation recital in Aeolian Hall, after which she served as accompanist, played in a trio, performed on the radio, and began to teach.

In 1925 she returned to Puerto Rico to participate in a program in memory of her father, who had died two years earlier.[4] In 1927 she again returned home to teach at the Academia Católica of San Francisco Church (Old San Juan), where she played the organ and developed a children's choir. From 1929 to 1933, she taught music in various public schools in Puerto Rico. In 1933 she returned to the concert circuit, playing with the Russian cellist Bogumil Sycora in fourteen concerts, and playing with the Puerto Rican Symphony Orchestra under the direction of Manuel Tizol.[5] In 1935, she was the first woman to direct an opera performance in San Juan, when she directed Mascagni's <u>Cavalleria Rusticana</u> in the Municipal Theatre.[6] In recognition of her contribution to the music of Puerto Rico, she was awarded a virtuoso artist's diploma by the President of the Symphony, Judge Ignacio Carballiera and Manuel Tizol, director.[7] In 1935, she was named to the Board of Directors of the Puerto Rican Symphony Orchestra. Over the years, she toured the western hemisphere performing, and in 1955 she returned to New York where she has since served the Hispanic-American community.[8]

In 1970, in one of the most moving performances of her career, and certainly one of the most meaningful, Genoveva De Arteaga performed in Carnegie Recital Hall in a concert celebrating fifty years of professional life. From 1975 to 1977, she was chairman of the National Guild of Piano Teachers, and in the autumn of 1976 she represented the American College of Musicians' official people-to-people mission to Europe and the Soviet Union. While her career was exemplary, she was as much a product of the decade after the Spanish-American War as were those who were active during that period.

In addition to Arteaga, the children of Jesús Figueroa have carried on the traditions of that important period of transition. The five brothers, JOSÉ, KACHIRO, GUILLERMO, RAFAEL, and NARCISO were trained in Puerto Rico and in Paris, and when they were leaving Paris their teacher, Alfred Cortot of the Paris Conservatoire, suggested that they form an ensemble. Since that time, the world has been blessed with the music of the FIGUEROA QUINTET, a group which since 1968 has been officially recognized by the Government of Puerto Rico as an official performing group, the Ambassadors of Good Will of the island of Puerto Rico. As a group, the Figueroa Quintet have become world famous. As individuals they are equally proficient as soloists. José, for example, won the Sarasate Violin Prize upon graduation from the Real Conservatorio of Madrid, and they he studied at Paris, where he became a violin teacher and a member of the chamber orchestra of the Paris Conservatoire. He later was the first violinist and soloist of the Paris Symphony, and he won the Wieniawski Centenary competition.

Kachiro followed the footsteps of his older brother, José. He also studied at Madrid, where he also won the Sarasate Prize. He then studied at Paris, where he studied with Jacques Thibaud and Jacques Chailley. Kachiro has become director of the orchestra of the Institute of Culture of Puerto Rico. The next brother, Guillermo studied the viola at the Paris Conservatoire, and is presently a member of the faculty of the Conservatory of Music of Puerto Rico. Rafael studied violoncello at Paris, where he was a disciple of Pierre Fournier, Nadia Boulanger, and Oliver Messiaen. He was a member of the American Symphony Orchestra [New York], and he is presently a member of the Puerto Rican Symphony. Narciso won first prize in piano and chamber music at the Real Conservatorio of Madrid, and he studied under Cortot at Paris. He has become a distinguished composer, won many prizes, and is a member of the faculty of the Conservatory of Music of Puerto Rico.

The Figueroa Quintet presents a series of concerts in Puerto Rico and abroad annually. Aside from its indisputable musical excellence, it is unique in that its members are all brothers from a most distinguished musical family of Puerto Rico. In addition to this, they studied with a group of masters in Paris and Madrid with whom they created an

THE FIGUEROA QUINTET

aesthetic vision and a common technique which gave the ensemble an extraordinary homogeneity. Individually, each one has made his reputation at home and abroad as soloists and as members of various ensembles. In the last fifteen years the Figueroa Quintet has participated in cultural missions throughout Europe and the United States. Their chamber music tradition is now being carried on by their children, all graduates of the Juilliard School of Music, New York City,--the next Figueroa Quintet.

It is apparent that the decade after the Spanish-American War was an important period of transition for Puerto Rico. Yet, that period spawned a generation of musicians who not only were able to carry on the native musical and cultural traditions, but who brought light to a people who faced a future of darkness, to people who lived in a land faced with economic hardship, political uncertainty, and cultural change. They had a vision of greatness, a vision that succeeded in transcending the problems which faced the island. In the process they brought musical culture to thousands, even hundreds of thousands of people, not only in Puerto Rico but around the world. As a recent popular song exclaimed, they "lit up" the lives of a people whose lives were darkened by events beyond their control. Rather than being forgotten, they earned the right to be remembered with reverence, as important characters in a most difficult period in the cultural life of Puerto Rico. It is to those musicians that this book is dedicated.

NOTES

1. Affidavit No. 1048, signed by María Teresa Torruella, Pianist and Music Teacher at the former Academia Arteaga, dated January 20, 1934. Her report shows that she studied mostly with her mother.

2. Notice from the Oficina de la Presidenta, signed by Mother R.A. Arsuaja, R.S.C.J., Colegio Universitaria del Sagrado Corazón.

3. "El Conservatorio de música de San Juan de Puerto Rico," Puerto Rico Ilustrado, XXV/1279 (September 8, 1934), 10. The date is on the certificate signed by Carl Heim, President, August Fraemcke, Director, and John S. Meyer, Secretary.

4. El Mundo, (May 1, 1925).

5. Program in Mrs. De Arteaga's Scrapbook.

6. El Mundo, (December 21, 1935), n.p., article in her scrapbook.

7. Sebastián Dalmau y Canet, "Nuestros Valores Musicales: Genoveva de Arteaga como artista y como profesora," Ambito, II/1 (September, 1934), 8.

8. She is the subject of a book, Latinoamericana en dos mil conciertos by Hernando Merchand.

BIBLIOGRAPHY

Abad, José Ramón. Puerto Rico en la feria exposición de Ponce en 1882. San Juan: Editorial Coquí, 1967.

Alegría, José S. "Las Retretas," Revista del Instituto de Cultura Puertorriqueña, II/2 (January-March, 1959), 23-24.

"Antonio Paoli, breves datos biográficos," Nosotros, I/4 (March-April, 1966), 11.

Araez y Ferrando, Ramón. Historia del ciclón del día de San Ciriaco. San Juan: Imp. Heraldo Español, 1905.

Arbor Day in Puerto Rico. San Juan: Department of Education of Puerto Rico, November 15, 1910.

Astol, José Eugenio, "José Ignacio Quintón músico," Puerto Rico Ilustrado, XXVIII/1427 (July 17, 1937), 26, 53.

Ateneo Puertorriqueño. San Juan: Talleres Gráficos Interamericanos, Inc., 1966.

Babín, María Teresa. La cultura de Puerto Rico. San Juan: Instituto de Cultura Puertorriqueña, 1970

Balseiro, José A., "Dos danzas de Rafael Balseiro Dávila," Revista del Instituto de Cultura Puertorriqueña, VI/20 (July-September, 1963), 22-23.

_____, "In memoriam," Puerto Rico Ilustrado, XXVIII/1545 (October 28, 1939), 3.

Berbusse, Edward J. The United States in Puerto Rico, 1898-1900. Chapel Hill: University of North Carolina Press, 1966.

Bragg, David Alwyn. The Teaching of Music Concepts in the Elementary Schools of Puerto Rico. Tallahasse, Florida: Florida State University Ph.D. dissertation, 1971.

Brau, María M. Island in the Crossroads: The History of Puerto Rico. Garden City, N.Y.: Doubleday Zenith Book, 1968.

Cadman, Charles Wakefield, "Music in Puerto Rico," The Music News, (May 18, 1939), 11, 22.

Callejo Ferrer, Fernando. "Braulio Dueño Colón, Flautista-Compositor," El Mes histórico, I/8 (March, 1935), 7-11.

_____. Música y Músicos Portorriqueños. San
    Juan: Tip. Cantero Fernández & Co., 1915.

_____, Música y Músicos Puertorriqueños. ed
    by Amaury Veray. San Juan: Editorial Coquí, 1971.

Campos Parsi, Héctor. Música, VII, La Gran Enciclopedia de
    Puerto Rico. San Juan [Madrid: C. Corredera], 1976.

Carreras, Carlos M. Hombres y mujeres de Puerto Rico. México:
    Editorial Orión, 1957.

Carteles [Havana], XXII/37 (September 30, 1934).

Caso, Fernando H. Héctor Campos Parsi in the History of
    Twentieth Century Music of Puerto Rico. Bloomington:
    Indiana University Master of Music thesis, 1972.

The Catholic Choirmaster, VII/4 (October, 1921).

Centenario de la Fundación del Ateneo Puertorriqueño, 1876-1976.
    San Juan: Ateneo Puertorriqueño, 1976.

Certamenes del Ateneo Puertorriqueño, 1877-1970. n.d.

Chavier Arévalo, Arístides. Articles in the Archivo General de
    Puerto Rico Reference Room, Vols. 1, 3, 5, 6, 9.

_____. "Porto Rican Musical Art. El arte
    musical Puertorriqueño, su desarrollo y evolución hasta el
    presente," in El Libro de Puerto Rico. ed. by Eugenio
    Fernández y Garcia. San Juan: El Libro Azul Publishing
    Co., 1923, pp. 775-785.

_____. Siluetas Musicales. Ponce: Imp. El
    Día, 1926.

Chiles, Paul Nelson. The Puerto Rican Press Reactions to the
    United States, 1888-1898. Philadelphia: University of
    Pennsylvania Press, 1944.

Coll y Toste, Cayetano. Prehistoria de Puerto Rico. San Juan:
    Tipografía Boletín Mercantil, 1907.

Colón, Edmundo. Datos sobre la agricultura de Puerto Rico antes
    de 1898. San Juan: Cantero Fernández & Co., 1930.

Compositores Puertorriqueños. San Juan: Archivo General de
    Puerto Rico unpublished booklet, n.d.

Cortijo, Alahija L. La música popular y los músicos celebres de la América Latina. Barcelona: Casa Editorial Mauuci, 1903.

Course of Study and Duties of Teachers, 1901-2. San Juan: Department of Education. San Juan News Press, 1901.

La Critica [San Juan, P.R.], I/1 (June 15, 1915), 40.

Dalmau y Canet, Sebastián. "Nuestros valores musicales: Genoveva de Arteaga como artista y como profesora," Ambito, II/1 (September, 1934), 8-9.

Daubon, José Antonio. Cosas de Puerto Rico II. San Juan: Tip. La Correspondencia, 1904-5.

Dávila, Arturo V. "El platero Domingo de Andino (1737-1820), maestro de música de Campeche," Revista del Instituto de Cultura Puertorriqueña, V/16 (July-September, 1962), 36-38.

_____. "José Campeche, maestro de música," Revista del Instituto de Cultura Puertorriqueña, III/8 (July-September, 1960), 14-16.

Deliz, Monserrate. Scrapbooks. San Juan: Universidad de Puerto Rico, Salón de Música, 1933.

Dower, Catherine A., "The Afro-Caribbean Musical Legacy/Part One: The Music of Puerto Rico," Musart, XXVI/3 (Spring, 1974), 52-56.

_____, "Libraries With Music Collections in the Caribbean Area," Notes, XXXIV/1 (September, 1977), 27-28.

_____, "The Reaction of the Puerto Rican Musicians to the Spanish American War," Boletín de la Academia des Artes y Ciencias de Puerto Rico, XIII/1-2 (January, 1978), 45-67.

_____, "Highlights in the Career of Julio Carlos Arteaga (1865-1923)," Revista Euterpe, (April, 1979), 35, 40.
_____, "Ramón Morlá, Composer-Organist," Sacred Music, CVI/2 (Summer, 1979), 15-20.

_____, "Julio Carlos De Arteaga, (1865-1923)," Revista Euterpe, VIII (October-November, 1979), 16-19, 22, 23.

_____, "Puerto Rican Music following the Spanish American War, 1898-1910), Revista/Review Interamericano, VIII/4 (Summer, 1979), 620-628.

_____, "Four Prominent Puerto Rican Women Musicians Following the Spanish American War," Revista Euterpe, IX (January, 1980), 15-18.

_____, "They Kept a Tradition Going," Dateline...Puerto Rico, U.S.A., II/1 (July-August, 1980), 23-25.

_____, "Monsita Ferrer," in The International Encyclopedia of Women Composers. (Aaron Cohen ed.) New York: Bowker, 1981.

_____, "The Arteaga Family's Gift: Classics for Puerto Rico," Dateline Puerto Rico, U.S.A., II/5 (March-April, 1981), 28-29.

_____, "Bearer of a Musical Tradition, Dateline Puerto Rico, U.S.A., III/2 (Fall, 1981), 41-2.

_____, "Quintón Bridges Centuries," Dateline Puerto Rico, U.S.A., III/3 (Winter, 1981), 38.

Dueño, Manuel. Braulio Dueño Colón Estudio Biográfico. Bayamón: Imp. Moreno Hijo, 1944.

Dueño Colón Braulio. "Estudio sobre la danza Puertorriqueña," in Brújula, III/9-10 (November, 1937), 17-21, in De semántica musical y otros estudios. ed. by Angel Mergal Llera.

_____ And Manuel Fernández Juncos. Canciones Escolares. New York: Silver Burdett & Co., 1924.

"El Conservatorio de Música de San Juan de Puerto Rico," Puerto Rico Ilustrado, XXV/1279 (September 8, 1934), 10.

"El Gran Tenor Puertorriqueño, Antonio Paoli," El Carnaval, IX/17 (March 29, 1908), 16.

"El Origen del Teatro Tapia," Revista gráfica de Puerto Rico, V/51 (July, 1971), 58.

"Elisa Tavárez Colom," Nosotros, II/1 (May-June, 1968), 15.

"Elisa Tavárez de Storer, Estudio," La Democracia, XXVIII/7792 (February 16, 1917), 3, and XXVIII/7793 (February 17, 1917), 2.

Elisa Tavárez Estudio Biográfico. San Juan: Departamento de
     Instrucción Pública, 1958.

Escuela, IV/18 (December 7, 1953). San Juan: Departamento de
     Instrucción.

"Evocando a Rafael Balseiro Dávila: Octubre 23, 1929-1939"
     Puerto Rico Ilustrado, XXVIII/1545 (October 28, 1939), 1.

Fernández Juncos, Manuel, "Una precioso estudio sobre música
     religiosa," Cervantes, Revista Decenal de Literatura,
     Ciencias y Artes. IV/23 (July 10, 1908), 1-4.

"Fernando Callejo," Puerto Rico Ilustrado, I/10 (May 8, 1910),
     13.

Fitzmaurice, Robert M. Music Education in Puerto Rico: A
     Historical Survey with guidelines for an exemplary
     curriculum. Tallahassee, Florida: Florida State University
     Ph.D. dissertation, 1970.

Garrido, Pablo. Esotería y fervor populares de Puerto Rico.
     Madrid: Ediciones Cultura Hispanica, 1952.

"Genoveva de Arteaga de Dalmau," Handbook of the Puerto Rican
     Community [El Libro Puertorriqueño]. Federico Ribes Tovar
     Edition.

Gil de Prann, Josefina. Typical Christmas Customs in Puerto
     Rico. San Juan: Imp. Correo Dominical, 1929.

Gómez Canedo, Lino. Los Archivos Históricos de Puerto Rico.
     Barcelona: M. Pareja, 1964.

Gómez Tejera, Carmen, "Arte Puertorriqueño," Programma de
     Español II. Hato Rey, P.R.: Editorial del Departamento de
     Instrucción Pública, 1952, pp. 95-109.

Handbook of the Puerto Rican Community [El Libro
     Puertorriqueño]. Federico Ribes Tovar Edition.

Hermida, Francisco and Conde Kostia, "Paoli en la Habana," The
     Puerto Rico Herald, VIII/12 (September 28, 1901), 12.

"Hispanoamericanos Ilustres," Espiritisimo [Caracas], III/36
     (April, 1969), 2.

Hostos, Adolfo de. Historia de San Juan ciudad murada. San Juan:
     Instituto de Cultura Puertorriqueña, 1966.

Infiesta, Alejandro. La Exposición de Puerto Rico. San Juan: Imp. del Boletín Mercantil, 1895.

"José I. Quintón," Puerto Rico Ilustrado, XXXVI/1861 (December 8, 1945), 21.

"Julio C. De Arteaga," Revista Musical Euterpe, (May 6, 1972).

Junta Directiva y Presidentes de Secciones. San Juan: Ateneo Puertorriqueño, 1909.

Labarth, Pedro Juan, "Elisa Tavárez--Angel de Paz," Puerto Rico Ilustrado, XVI/1355 (February 22, 1936), 17, 22.

Lamoutte, Sylvia Maria. Biografías Cortas de Compositores Puertorriqueños. San Juan, P.R., 1971.

Matos Bernier, Félix, "La música en Puerto Rico," Isla de arte. San Juan: Imp. La Primavera, 1907, 229-235.

Mayer-Serra, Otto, ed. Música y Músicos de Latina America. México: Editorial Atlante, 1947, Vol. 2.

Merchand, Hernando. Latinoamerica en dos mil conciertos. New York: Unida Printing Co., 1974.

Mixer, Knowlton. Porto Rico: history and conditions, social, economic, and political. New York: MacMillan, 1926.

Montañez, Rafael. "José Ignacio Quintón," Puerto Rico Ilustrado, XLII/2180 (February 2, 1952), 4-5.

_____, "Los aniversarios memorables: Recordando a Rafael Balseiro Dávila," Puerto Rico Ilustrado, XXVIII/1545 (October 28, 1939), 2, 57.

"La mujer de Borinqueña," Revista Musical Euterpe, (August, 1972), 18.

Mulet, Elaine, "Dos músicos al encuentro de un tesoro," El Mundo, LVI/84 (May 11, 1975), 4-5.

Muñoz, María Luisa, "La educación musical en Puerto Rico," Educación, XIII/10 (November, 1963), 107-114.

_____, La música en Puerto Rico: Panorama histórico-cultural. Sharon, Conn.: Troutman Press, 1966.

_____, "La música religiosa en Puerto Rico," Educación, XIII/10 (November, 1963), 25-38.

_____, "Music Education in Puerto Rico," Music Educators Journal, XXXIX (April-May, 1953), 56-7.

_____, "Puerto Rico and Its Music," Music Educators Journal, XXXIX (January, 1953), 51.

Negrón Muñoz, Angela. Mujeres de Puerto Rico desde el período de colonización hasta el primer tercio del siglo XX. San Juan: Imp. Venezuela, 1935.

Nemmers, Erwin Esser. Twenty Centuries of Catholic Church Music. Milwaukee: Bruce Publishing Co., 1949.

Orrigo, Iris. Images and Shadows. New York: Harcourt Brace, Javanovich, Inc., 1970.

Ortiz, Yvette. La canción de arte Puertorriqueña. San Juan: Instituto de Cultura Puertorriqueña, 1975.

Pardo de Casablanca, Coloma. "Composición Musical Puertorriqueña," Puerto Rico Ilustrado, XXXVI/1861 (November 24, 1945), 21, 72.

Pasarell, Emilio J. "El Centenario de los conciertos de Adelina Patti y Luis Moreau Gottschalk en Puerto Rico," Revista del Instituto de Cultura Puertorriqueña, II/2 (January-March, 1959), 52-55.

_____. Ensayos y otros artículos. San Juan: Editorial Cordillera, 1968.

_____. Esculcando el Siglo XIX en Puerto Rico. Barcelona: Rumbos, 1967.

_____. Orígenes y desarrollo de la afición teatral en Puerto Rico. Rio Piedras: Editorial Universitaria [Universidad de Puerto Rico], 1951, 1967, 2 vols.

Pedreira, Antonio A. Bibliografía Puertorriqueña (1493-1930). Madrid: Editorial Hernando, 1932.

The Puerto Rico Journal, I/1 (December 23, 1903), 3.

Puerto Rico Musical, Revista de Música, I/1 (February 15, 1906).

Regiment Orders/Special Orders Puerto Rico Provisional Infantry Regiment. June 1901 to December 1901. National Archives Navy and Old Army Division. [R.G. 395: Entry 5863].

Report of the Department of the Interior for the Fiscal Year
    Ended June 30, 1907, I. Washington, D.C. Government
    Printing Office, 1908.

Romeu, José A. "Don Rafael Balseiro," Puerto Rico Ilustrado,
    XXVIII/1545 (October 28, 1939), 4.

Roosevelt, Theodore. Colonial Policies of the United States. New
    York: Arno Press and the New York Times, 1970.

Rosa-Nieves y Esther M. Melón. Biografías Puertorriqueñas:
    Perfil histórico de un pueblo. Sharon, Conn.: Troutman
    Press, 1970.

Sáez, Antonio. El Teatro en Puerto Rico: notas para su historia.
    Río Piedras: Editorial Universitaria [Universidad de
    Puerto Rico], 1950.

_____. "En el centenario de Ana Otero
    Hernández," Revista del Instituto de Cultura
    Puertorriqueña, IV/11 (April–June, 1961), 40–42.

Schauensee, Max de. "The Lion of Ponce," Opera News, XXXVI/20
    (April 8, 1972), 6–7.

Schwartz, Francis, "Antonio Paoli: He stormed the world of
    opera," San Juan Star Sunday Magazine, (April 11, 1971), 7.

Secretary's Register of Puerto Rico for 1903. San Juan: Louis Z.
    Tuzo & Co., 1903.

Stevenson, Robert M. A Guide to Caribbean Music History. Lima,
    Peru: Ediciones "CVLTVRA," 1975.

Tavárez, Elisa. Scrapbooks "Desde 1900," "Año 1924," "Año 1933,"
    "Año 1958," and "1956–1959." in the Archivo General de
    Puerto Rico, Sección de música.

Thompson, Annie Figueroa. An Annotated Bibliography of Writings
    About Music in Puerto Rico. Ann Arbor: Music Library
    Association, 1975. No. 12, M.L.A. Index and Bibliography
    Series.

_____. Puerto Rican Newspapers and Journals of
    the Spanish Colonial Period as Source Materials for
    Musicological Research: An Analysis of Their Music
    Content. [The Florida State University Ph.D. , 1980], Ann
    Arbor, Michigan: University Microfilms International, 1980.

Thompson, Donald, "Music in Puerto Rico," Musical America, LXXX/8 (July, 1960), 19-23, 26-28.

_____, "Nineteenth Century Musical Life in Puerto Rico," Unpublished manuscript, August, 1973.

_____, "Puerto Rico--Art Music," The New Grove Dictionary of Music and Musicians, XV. London: Macmillan Publishers Ltd., 1980, p. 443.

Tooker, Helen V. "Puerto Rico's Tenor," San Juan Review, III/3 (April, 1966), 4.

United States Congress. Congressional Record. Washington, D.C. Government Printing Office.

U.S. House Document, Vol. 49, No. 5152, 59th Congress, 2nd Session, Document No. 203.

U.S. House of Representatives Document No. 5557, 60th Congress, 2nd Session, Document No. 1204, 1908.

U.S. Senate Document, Vol. 33, No. 3875, 56th Congress, Document No. 363.

U.S. Senate Document, No. 4910, 59th Congress, 1st Session, Document No. 60, 1905.

U.S. Senate Document, No. 5070, 56th Congress, 2nd Session, Document No. 135.

U.S. Senate Document, No. 5393, 60th Congress, 2nd Session, Annual Report of the Governor of Puerto Rico, Document No. 578.

United States Volunteer, Puerto Rico Regiment Orders, Letters Sent MTD Battle/Infantry/A.G.O. War With Spain. Orders #16, #18, #26, #40, #41. [National Archives, Washington, D.C.].

Veray, Amaury. Elisa Tavárez Estudio biográfico. San Juan: Departamento de Instrucción Pública, 1958.

_____. "Fernando Callejo Ferrer," Revista del Instituto de Cultura Puertorriqueña, V/16 (July-September, 1962), 58-60.

_____. "La misión social de la danza de Juan Morel Campos," Revista del Instituto de Cultura Puertorriqueña, II/5 (October-December, 1959), 35-38.

_____. "Monsita Ferrer, Sonatina
Puertorriqueña para canto y esperanza," Revista del
Instituto de Cultura Puertorriqueña, V/7
(October-December), 10-12.

_____. "Presentación de José Ignacio
Quintón," Revista del Instituto de Cultura Puertorriqueña,
III/8 (July-September, 1960), 17-19.

_____. Vida y desarrollo de la danza
Puertorriqueña. San Juan: Carnegie Library Sala
Puertorriqueña, Unpublished manuscript, n.d.

Villarini, Awilda. A Study of Selected Puerto Rican Dances for
the Piano. [New York University Ph.D. dissertation, 1979],
Ann Arbor, Michigan: University Microfilms International,
1979.

NEWSPAPERS

Boletín Mercantil de Puerto Rico. 1839, 1841, 1842, 1899-1910.

La Correspondencia de Puerto Rico. 1905-1910, 1931.

La Democracia. 1901, 1911, 1915, 1917.

La Educación. 1909-1910.

El Baluarte. 1906.

El Carnaval. 1908.

El Día. 1901-1902, 1911-1913, 1915-1916, 1925.

El Diario de Puerto Rico. 1900.

El Diario-La Prensa. (January, 1972).

El Eco de la Policia Insular. 1901-1902.

El Mundo. 1925, 1931, 1935-1937, 1975.

El País. 1899, 1901-1902.

Espiritisimo. 1967.

La Gaceta del Gobierno de Puerto Rico. 1835, 1848.

The New York Times. 1877, 1899, 1903, 1910.

Official Gazette of Puerto Rico. 1909.

The Puerto Rico Eagle. 1909-1910, 1913.

The Puerto Rico Herald. 1901-1904.

The Puerto Rico Sun. 1903-1904.

The Puerto Rico Times. 1902.

The San Juan News. 1899, 1900-1904.

The San Juan Review. 1966.

201

CATHERINE DOWER, Professor of Music History at Westfield State College, Westfield, Massachusetts, graduated from Hamline University (A.B.) where she majored in music under Ernst Krenek, Smith College (M.A.) in musicology under Dr. Alfred Einstein and Ross Lee Finney, and The Catholic University of America (Ph.D.) where she studied with Dr. Pauline Alderman. She was a Visiting Scholar at the University of Southern California, studied at the University of Innsbruck, Austria, Pius X School of Liturgical Music, Solesmes Abbey, and Tanglewood, the Berkshire Music Center. She was on the faculty of the University of Massachusetts, Amherst, and a Visiting Associate Professor at Herbert Lehman College of the City University of New York (1970-71). She has articles published in MUSIC JOURNAL, MUSART, NOTES, REVISTA/REVIEW INTERAMERICANA, BOLETIN of the Academy of Arts and Sciences of Puerto Rico, of which she is a Corresponding Member, DATELINE, PUERTO RICO, U.S.A. of which she is on the Editorial Board, SACRED MUSIC, REVISTA EUTERPE, DIE MUSIK IN GESHCHITE UND GEGENWART, and THE NEW GROVE DICTIONARY OF MUSIC AND MUSICIANS, and editions of choral music (Alexander Broude, Inc.).

She has received the Distinguished Service award from Westfield State College three times, (1979, '81, '83), was named Professor of the Year (1975), and was presented a plaque from the Springfield Symphony Orchestra Association (1982). She is President of the Holyoke Council for Human Understanding (1982-83), Chairman of the Holyoke Chapter of the Irish American Cultural Institute (1981-), a member of the Board of Directors of many organizations including the Hispanic Institute, Inc. of Holyoke, a member of the Academia Interamericana de Puerto Rico, and her biography appears in several biographical sources.